"D.W. Brown is one of the most insightful and best acting teachers around."

—MEG LIEBERMAN, Emmy Award–winning casting director

"D.W. Brown guided me and how to work with actors. I've incorporated the basic premise he works under and he gave me a lot of tips."

—SAM RAIMI, director, *Spider-Man*

"Working with D.W. Brown is the most important thing I have done for my career."

—SHARON CASE, Emmy Award–winning actress, *Young and The Restless*

"As one of the premiere teachers in Hollywood on the craft of acting, D.W. Brown teaches how to be great and what it takes in this business to be successful. No one knows acting or teaches it better than D.W. Brown!"

—DAVID ROGERS, Emmy Award–winning director/editor, *Seinfeld*, *The Office*

"Over the 30 years or so I've been producing, the Joanne Baron/D.W. Brown Studio has etched a place of renown for the skills they teach and care most about—performance. This has to be an exceptional book by an exceptional person."

—DOUG CLAYBOURNE, producer, *Fast and The Furious*, *North Country*, *The Mask of Zorro*

"Even if you're not an actor, but a writer or director or AD, this book gives you insight into the actor's perspective and psychology. It will help you communicate with actors as well as re-approach your own craft from a new perspective."

—CHAD GERVICH, writer/producer: *After Lately*, *Cupcake Wars*; author: *How to Manage Your Agent; Small Screen, Big Picture*

"I remember feeling a sense of security from D.W. He provided an atmosphere within which the insecure novice actor could safely strive explore, and even fail."

—ROBIN WRIGHT, actress, *Forest Gump, Ho*

D1557492

Insider Tips for Delivering
A Great Performance Every Time

....

YOU CAN ACT

ON

CAMERA

....

D. W. BROWN

MICHAEL WIESE PRODUCTIONS

Published by Michael Wiese Productions
12400 Ventura Blvd. #1111
Studio City, CA 91604
(818) 379-8799, (818) 986-3408 (Fax)
mw@mwp.com
www.mwp.com
Manufactured in the United States
of America

Cover design by Johnny Ink. johnnyink.com
Interior design by Debbie Berne
Copyediting by David Wright

This book was set in Garamond Premiere Pro
and Whitney.

Library of Congress Cataloging-in-Publication Data
Brown, D. W., 1956-
 You can act on camera : insider tips for delivering a great
performance every time / D. W. Brown.
    pages cm
 ISBN 978-1-61593-233-7
1. Motion picture acting. 2. Television acting. I. Title.
PN1995.9.A26B97 2015
791.4502'8—dc23
                        2015015516

CONTENTS

....

INTRODUCTION

....

No matter the medium, good acting is good acting, and the difference between what's good for the stage and preferable for a camera is a matter of nuance. If your style of acting is naturalistic, engaging your emotional belief in a scene's circumstances and maintaining uncertainty for how it will unfold, the difference is often little more than the theater's requirement of vocal projection and the occasional "cheat" to be seen. Still, an actor and a camera do have a special relationship and the conditions designed for recording a performance have their own unique challenges.

This book will address that nuance and those challenges. It lays out thirty-two key principles for the creation of an effective performance on camera and offers advice on how to surmount the particular obstacles associated with attempting to rise to the occasion on a set. Also included are interviews with very smart professionals who offer insights and practical advice on getting your best work captured.

I advocate here, as in my first book, *You Can Act: A Complete Guide for Actors*, an internal style of acting (associated with Stanislavski) that urges an artist to live through their performance, as opposed to an external approach whose primary concern is to demonstrate behaviors for the benefit of the audience. (You can see the extreme of the external style in silent films.) The internal approach is, by far, the prevailing style for current film and television work, but this is not to say that I believe an actor should be limited to portrayals straight from their own personalities or cut themselves off from the many wonderful non-naturalistic presentations possible. I only encourage that the horse to be kept in front of the cart with a prevailing spirit of emotional truthfulness and a tilt toward subtlety.

When acting first appeared on film it was called a new art and generated a theory that these works induced in their audiences something of the experience of a dream. It makes sense. The reason you can watch a character climbing a mountain in one moment and then instantly cut to them taking a bath in the next without becoming alarmingly disoriented is because you experience the same sort thing of every night. In this way, an actor acting on camera does well to consider themselves participants in these dreams and therefore can enter into this world of intimacy and rawness as naturally as a second home.

Good acting is good acting. It's the joy in playing pretend, the passion to inspire, and the discipline to serve material consistently and successfully. Whether it's performed for the eyes of hundreds or the single lens of the camera, the actor's calling is to find their way into another open heart.

THE 32 PRINCIPLES
OF ACTING ON CAMERA

....

1. GET YOUR LINES COLD

The single most important act of preparation for your role is to get your lines down cold. You'll think you know them and then on a chaotic set with the pressure and the two new things you're supposed to do . . . nope, they start slipping away. Don't memorize inflections, but know your words by rote so perfectly you could rattle them off while falling down stairs.

"Be conscious where you should be conscious, so you can be unconscious where you should be unconscious." —T. S. Eliot

2. TIGHTEN EVERYTHING

Everything being recorded that could be used in the final product should be kept clipping along and free of dead spots. When an event happens, react and speak as you're taking it in. Rarely pause while speaking. Engage and compress.

"If you take any activity and push it as far as it will go, push it to the wildest edge of edges, then you force it into the realm of magic." —Tom Robbins

3. DON'T SAY MUCH

React and drive your basic Actions, but don't explain or make points or address yourself to people's intellects. Attempts to communicate information from your brain to their brain will thin the voice and create facial tension that gets magnified in the close-up. Let the information take care of itself. In every screenwriting class the point is made to "show, don't tell," and, with this in mind, accept that the information you render is of very low value.

"Be not a slave of words." —Thomas Carlyle

4. FIND YOUR ROLE AND BE THAT A LOT

Everyone involved in a production has a job and you have yours. The story is trying to be something and you must put your desires in line with helping it be that thing. It may want you to create tension or it may want you to create peace. It always wants the situation of the lead to be clearer.

"Are you willing to own that probably the only good reason for your existence is not what you are going to get out of life, but what you are going to give to life?" —Henry van Dyke

5. MATCH AS MATCH CAN

Your best work from one portion of a take can be cut together with the best portion from another take and played as one continuum provided those two takes have no jarring physical differences or differences in points of escalation or quietude. It is therefore to your advantage (and the filmmakers who will appreciate you) to maintain a consistency for these things from take to take. Reinvest in the values, but put that cup down at the same place each time you run the scene.

To be conscientious about this while acting will in no way diminish your imaginative involvement (it may even improve it), but do not be a slave to continuity. The truth of the moment must always and absolutely dictate your behavior.

"Do what you have to do, so you can do what you want to do." —*Denzel Washington*

6. STAY FRESH

The key element in most work on camera is to appear as if real events are taking place for the first time. Whether big things or small things, the audience wants to have the sense they're watching something unique in the history of the universe, like each moment of actual life. We don't want the feeling that you're ahead of what's unfolding in any way.

Whatever it is you have to do (or not do) to give that impression, do that.

"To understand is almost the opposite of existing." —*George Poulet*

7. ACT SMALLER THAN THE SIZE OF THE SHOT

Calibrate your animation and volume to the framing. Ask the Director of Photography where you're framed and notice where the boom mic is being placed, then gesture and speak at a volume minimized to well under that.

"Speak your truth quietly and clearly." —*Max Ehrmann*

8. BE IT, DON'T SELL IT

Walk your walk, and win through the weight of what you're about, not your chatter. Vibe the other characters, as if communicating telepathically. Convey what is essential through a relaxed sharing of your life force. Happy about it or not, they get you.

"All paths lead to the same goal, to communicate to others what we really are." —Pablo Neruda

9. LOOK THEM IN THE EYE AND TELL THE TRUTH

Seek to have steady looks and a consistent, fluid channel to express the essence of your Action.

Typically you want to look into the eye of the off-camera person that is closest to the lens, and not flit glances, as you would normally, to their other eye and down to their mouth. You also don't want to look as much as you might normally at the other people in the scene who you're not talking with at that moment. Avoid checking in with how those secondary characters are receiving what's going on, unless, of course, they've just gotten big news.

"Let there be truth between us two forevermore." —Ralph Waldo Emerson

10. PUT IN RESTING MOMENTS

To move and speak at the same time is an important admonition to actors, but when working for the camera, it's good to have a sense for where an editor might want to cut. For instance, when you enter a room or a car, pause before speaking so that they can cut to the other characters registering your arrival.

When someone opposite you finishes speaking, take your time to get a full charge of response energy (even if it would be odd to do so in normal conversation), so you can then let it all pour out in a fast stream. They can always cut out the flat spot before you speak. You don't want to overlap dialogue when only one person is in the frame.

"Use time: go smoothly through its spaces to the center of opportunity."
—Baltasar Gracián

11. HAVE SOMETHING PHYSICAL GOING ON

Don't let the unreality of the set prevent you from conducting yourself as a human being. Interact with the physical world. Get very handy with a prop, an aspect of costume or jewelry, and enter the scene dealing with it as would be logical. Continue to manage or even toy with it during the scene (if it isn't distracting).

When drinking, eating, dressing, or engaged in any of these types of normal life behaviors, don't allow yourself to think about them. Just go on automatic and let your body do as it's done thousands of times before.

"Simplicity and naturalness are the truest marks of distinction."
—Somerset Maugham

12. DEVELOP THE CHARACTER IN YOUR BODY, RELEASE IT THROUGH YOUR EYES

All the analysis you do is for the purpose of finding a way to embody a character: Do they live in your forehead, your chest, or your low belly? Do they resemble a specific animal? Your character wants contact with the world.

"You do not have to walk on your knees for a hundred miles through the desert, repenting. You only have to let the soft animal of your body love what it loves." —Mary Oliver

13. SPEAK AS FAST AS YOU CAN, ACT AS SLOWLY AS YOU CAN

Rip quickly through your dialogue. Tend to speak as fast as it's possible to speak while still using your vocalization to affect the heart of the other character.

"Let go of this everywhere and this something, in exchange for this nowhere and nothing." —The Cloud of Unknowing

14. ALWAYS BE ASSIMILATING

You might have been rewarded for appearing totally on top of it in life, but we hate people like that on camera. Even characters up for every challenge shouldn't be too sure of anything. Your best stuff is going to be when, whether saying lines or not, you're in the process of intensely trying to digest a singular truth.

Nobody cares if you understand, believe, or know what

to make of a situation, only how horrified, awestruck, or otherwise occupied in seeking your deepest feelings about it you are.

"We think and name in one world, we live and feel in another."
—*Marcel Proust*

15. POUR IT ALL INTO A SMALL SPACE

When acting on camera you want to project a narrowing focus. Feel free to offer up different planes of your face and respond to everything, but concentrate the energy of your will on an almost impossibly small spot, usually at the impossibly central spot (not a physical place) of the person you're addressing.

"The moment one gives close attention to anything, even a blade of grass, it becomes a mysterious, awesome, indescribably magnificent world in itself." —Henry Miller

16. ROUGH IT

Keep your performance unfinished and mussy. No matter how much rehearsal you've had, don't let your performance get too polished, clean, or wrapped up with a bow. Beware knowing what you're doing.

"The natural inheritance of everyone who is capable of spiritual life is an unsubdued forest where the wolf howls and the obscene bird of night chatters." —Henry James

17. BE PROFESSIONAL

Keep your agreements and be neither noticeably present nor noticeably absent from the set. Use discipline when not acting, so you can be wild when you are acting.

"Combine punctuality, efficiency, good nature, obedience, intelligence, and concentration with an unawareness of what is going to happen next, thus keeping yourself available for excitement." —John Gielgud

18. KEEP A SECRET

When playing romance or other deeply intimate relationships, you want to create the sense of a shared secret (the intensity of the secret is the intensity of the relationship), but it's also good to have personal secrets known only to yourself. Create complications with the other characters. Entertain the possibility you could reveal the truth of this secret at any moment and set off a bomb.

"Let Mystery have its place in you." —Henri Amiel

19. TALK SOFTLY

Watching a recorded fiction creates a magical world where intimacy among the characters becomes a given. This means it's nearly impossible to be too quiet when acting on camera. You can fail through a lack a connection to your stomach and poor follow-through, but as long as those things are present you can speak at a level barely audible, much quieter than you ever would in life (even to a crowd at a distance!), and it will be acceptable and wonderful.

"When two people understand each other in their inmost hearts, their words are sweet and strong, like the fragrance of orchids." —The I Ching

20. ONLY MOVE YOUR MOUTH

Often in extreme close-ups, and some wider shots of high intensity, you may be served by assuming a condition such that your entire body is totally unmoving (not frozen) except for your mouth. Nothing about you should animate except the basic mechanics of speaking and the activity of your internal desire to project your will.

"The Great Way has no gate. Clear water has no taste. The tongue has no bone. In complete stillness, a stone girl is dancing." —Seung Sahn

21. BE YOUR PURE SELF OR FIND A HOOK

Call it a hook or a thread or "a way in," but with the limited rehearsal time you're likely to have working on camera, if you're going to do a character different from yourself, you should find a specific behavior you can hold onto all the way through. It might be a way of walking or speaking or placing your tongue in your mouth. It could be you're always looking for a mysterious clue or one perfect soul. Find it and stay close to it and be open to whatever else it brings.

"All that is alive tends toward color, individuality, specificity, effectiveness, and opacity." —Johann Wolfgang von Goethe

22. THINK LOUDLY

For key moments without dialogue, especially in close-up,

make that voice in your head shout the Truth. Make it blare a command for you to take action or embrace a stark fact (i.e. "Stop her! You've got to stop her!" or "You will never see home again! Never!").

"Facing it, always facing it; that's the way to get through. Face it!"
—Joseph Conrad

23. DO NOTHING

There will be times that the best performance you can give is a blank one upon which the audience can, without contamination, project what they want to be there. Respect the power of their connection to the full context of what's been presented to them up to this point (including what will be added in postproduction) and, far beyond this, what they bring to it of their own. Nothing you can act will be as remotely strong as what they invest on their own.

"Be a sheet of paper with nothing on it. Be a piece of ground where nothing is growing, a place where something might be planted: a seed, possibly, from the Absolute." —Rumi

24. BE FULLY SEEN

A camera sees everything, so you might as well let go and let it in. Show it all your doubts and imperfections and shameful qualities, because there are no shameful qualities, there are only people. And people are interesting.

"If I reveal myself without worrying about how others will respond, some will care and others may not; but who can love me if no one knows me? I must risk it or live alone." —Sheldon Kopp

25. BE LUCKY

Get a charm, an incantation, or some self-esteem perhaps, but find a way to get yourself on the good side of the universe. Maybe you're already in the groove or maybe every challenging and complicating thing up to this point has only been to set you up for your big breakthrough. One thing is for sure, if you're reading this right now, you've got a chance.

"What helps luck is a habit of watching for opportunities, of having a patient, but curious mind, of sacrificing one's ease or vanity, of uniting a love of detail to foresight, and of passing through hard times bravely and cheerfully." —Charles Victor Cherbuliez

26. GO EASY

You have to find a way to put all the pressure and madness of this world aside when you enter the imaginative world. You owe it that.

"The butterfly doesn't take it is as a personal achievement, he just disappears through the tree. It wasn't in a greedy mood you saw the light that belongs to everybody." —Jack Kerouac

27. FLOW

Establish for yourself what you're expressing in each section of a scene so that, whether actually delivering lines or not, you know the basic message you're sending out. When you're performing and feel insecure, act that thing even more.

There is no brake on this ride, only an ejection lever ... and don't you dare touch it. Welcome difficulties. They shake things up and open new doors. There's no floating along passively with flow, only a leaning forward in openness. And the moment you're sure you've got it, you can be sure you don't.

"The hearing of the ears is one thing and understanding something else. But the hearing of the spirit is not limited to the ear or to the mind and demands the emptiness of all the faculties. When the faculties are empty, then the whole being listens. There is then a direct contact of what is right there before you that can never be heard with the ear or understood with the mind." —Chuang-Tzu

28. RUN DEEP

Stir yourself to your foundations. Odors, tastes, and skin sensations are good for doing this. Send messages to yourself that you're all in, even admitting you don't really know what that is.

"In each of us there is another whom we do not know. He speaks to us in dreams and tells us how differently he sees us from the way we see ourselves." —Carl Jung

29. GO SIMPLER

Whatever you're doing, do it simpler. Be ruthless about stripping one more layer away. Get in even closer contact with the world, express yourself in a still plainer way, be all the more in your body.

"Human life is meant for a little austerity. We have to purify our existence; that is the mission of human life, because only then we will get spiritual realization and real pleasure, real happiness." —A. C. Bhaktivedanta

30. DIE AND BE REBORN

Every moment is new and waiting for you to surrender yourself to it without the husk of what you once were a moment before. Don't even think about wanting it any other way.

"It is almost as if you were frantically constructing another world while the world that you live in dissolves beneath your feet, and that your survival depends on completing this construction at least one second before the old habitation collapses." —Tennessee Williams

31. GET OUT OF THE WAY

Your work is to channel into a fiction and become as transparent as possible so your audience can clearly see the show through the opening you've created. They are seeking intimate contact with that world, like a lover who's been separated from their soul mate. You must remove yourself so they can share their secrets.

"To give up our imaginary position as the center, to renounce it, not only intellectually, but in the imaginative part of our soul, is to awaken to what is real and eternal, to see the true light and hear the true silence. To empty ourselves of our false divinity, to give up being the center of the world, to discern that all points in the world are equally centers and that the true center is outside the world, this is our free choice. Such consent is love. The face of this love is the love of our neighbor and the love of beauty." —Simone Weil

32. DO WHATEVER YOU HAVE TO DO

Make it happen. No excuses. Go hard . . . and let it come to you, both. Nobody cares what you have to do to get where you have to get, just that you do, and as long as it's properly recorded, you only have to get there once.

"You can have anything you want if you want it desperately enough. You must want it with an exuberance that erupts through the skin and joins the energy that created the world." —Sheila Graham

"ON THE DAY"
An Essay on Getting
Your Best Performance Recorded

....

"On the day" in filmmaking lingo refers to when you're actually there on the set and trying to make it happen. It's when all the elements are present, either set up and shooting, or in the immediate process of setting up to shoot. It isn't literal in that in the morning you can talk about something that's going to be shot later that same day saying, "They're delivering the crane after lunch, so we'll have it on the day." It's often used when referring to unanticipatable issues, the known unknowns and unknown unknowns, both artistic and technical, associated with recording material that can be used in the final product. On some shoots with a lot of moving parts, what happens on the day is going to include something of the sense of another expression, "the fog of war."

On the day is a special place. It's the proving ground where everything meets and must bow down in subservience to reality. Unimagined opportunities will emerge and things thought to be a slam-dunk become a complicated mess or altogether impossible. You might get a cool idea to do a thing with a thing, but then on the day it won't work because there's a problem with the lighting or the sound or the desired framing or something's been added so that part of the original script no longer makes sense. It could be that the edge of the counter is two inches too close to get clearance with your bag, or maybe the costume is so stiff it looks weird when you sit, or if you can see the bruise, it doesn't make sense that you'd just ignore it, and on and on.

I once had to deal with an interior security window in a school that was passing for a jail visiting area, and it wasn't until on the day we discovered that, because the phones were just props and didn't actually work, the actors couldn't hear each other through the heavy glass. Because of this, in playing the scene the actors had to take on a concern for not turning their heads in a way that would reveal the wires to the earbuds they were wearing.

It might be there's too little rehearsal or because an actor you're playing opposite changes things subsequent to rehearsal, but there will be plenty of challenging situations arising between actors on the day. I was acting in a film where I said a line with a particular legal term and the actress in the scene then responded with such obvious alarm it made it silly for the actor playing her husband to deliver his line explaining the gravity of the situation. I watched the poor guy squirm for a while before pushing through his discomfort to delicately point this out, and I wish I had a happier ending for this story, but his remark was not especially well received by the actress who blustered and insisted her character would certainly know what the term meant. I personally thought her choice misguided and her desire to be seen as intelligent a lost opportunity to instead show her character's innocence (a quality vastly more endearing than intelligence). But she was the star and carried herself as such and the director stepped in and told the actor to cut his line.

The point is, on the day you have to be prepared for all kinds of things to go sideways. It's all part of the adventure. Maybe you can compromise and get part of what you wanted or maybe you'll have to abandon your plan altogether. You'll have to decide whether to speak up and try to finesse or force what you had in mind through the obstacles, or whether to abandon it altogether and maintain your faith that there'll be wonderful opportunities revealing themselves in the future. Wonderful opportunities that are less likely to reveal themselves if you're still tortured by what you had to give up.

Not only will there be surprises out of the blue, but there's also going to be stuff being done just as it was described in the script that you didn't grasp the reality of actually doing until you were there and everyone was getting ready to shoot. You might have read where it said a rat crawls up your arm and sniffs your ear or that your dead body is discovered, but it's another thing to keep it together when that little furry devil starts going after the peanut butter they put behind your ear or when they start sprinkling live maggots on you (as they once did with my wife).

With nearly every situation on the day you almost certainly will be forced to deal with a monster that looms over everything: TIME. The production of a film or television show has some of the characteristics of a military operation, and it's been said that every military defeat can be described with the expression, "too late." You're losing the light, you're losing the location, you're losing the child actor who can only work a certain number of hours. You might get a great idea for something on the day, but it was only a great idea if you'd had it in time to work it out in preproduction, because now you just don't have that time. Oh, the pain.

With low-budget projects the time squeeze is almost always nuts, but even with productions that have huge budgets there are going to be situations where you have unbelievable time pressure. Stars may have professional or personal obligations taking them away, weather may be changing, hard release dates must be met, and the reality is only a small percentage of projects spend their money on making time a luxury. Nearly everyone spreads the margin as thin as they can so every penny shows up on the screen.

MAKE IT WORK ON THE FLY

Because of the many unexpected and unique contingencies that come up on the day, the skill for finding ad hoc solutions and the ability to adapt to issues as they arise out of the moment is one of the most useful talents an actor working on camera can develop. There are all manner of wild cards you'll be asked to manage.

It may be a last-minute rewrite or maybe the director has decided to go for a particular effect and now you're being asked to stand up and walk over by the window because, regardless of whether it makes sense for your character to do that, they want to establish that it's raining outside or the production values are better over there. It doesn't matter. They want you to do it and it's on you to implement the direction.

This skill is really just an extension of the actor's basic job description—to make an entire role work. If you have to betray another character in a scene, you've got to come up with a way to emotionally support that behavior, perhaps as an act of revenge or maybe by making your character a psychopath. If your character says something foolish, then it falls on you to justify this, maybe by having a low I.Q. or by being drunk. The particular challenge on the day is for an actor to compress that process to within minutes, perhaps seconds.

If you're asked to stand up and go to the window, you have to be able to quickly catalog your options and select the best one. It could be your character is not being so directly accusatory as you planned and is instead going to the window to demonstrate that these are simply inarguable facts being laid out; or it's possible you want to check the weather because someone you love is driving on the freeway (the audience won't know that, of course, but they can nevertheless sense you have a genuine purpose); or maybe your character's situation in life has become so burdensome that the moment prior to this move put you over the brink and you feel compelled to look out the window and catch your breath.

An actor has to constantly think and live outside the box. You must not fall too much in love with the way you visualized things happening. On the day, when your plan must be changed, you must free yourself from your natural inclination toward "anchor bias" and "confirmation bias." These are the strong tendencies we all have to develop beliefs in support of prior beliefs and to resist change. In formulating the best adaptation, you'll first need to overcome your clingy affection for what you thought was going to be the case and replace it with a willingness to "murder your darlings."

When test subjects are hooked up to a polygraph and shown ambiguous pictures (e.g., something that could either be a duck or a rabbit), some people will show more stress response than others. (Republicans tend to be more stressed than Democrats.) It seems this is just the way we're built as individuals and if you're one of those people who like things more definite, then you're probably going to be more resistant to changing your plan. Knowing this about yourself, you'll have to especially compensate for that and aspire to be the loosest, most easy-breezy adaptable actor possible.

It'll be to your benefit if you can maintain a clear head and a philosophy of flexibility, accepting this necessity to think on your feet as a constant factor in the undertaking you've chosen. I recommend approaching every project with pluck, spunk, pep, and good humor; and, when you begin to feel your teeth grinding because something must be lost and it's fallen upon you to put something wonderful in its place, reflect with gratitude on the fact that these are the kinds of problems you have.

I'm not saying it won't be aggravating and at times heart-breaking to lose something you loved about a scene. I once heard an actor in their pain of having to give up some little bit of character business say, "That's why I wanted to do this character in the first place!" But, come on. Steven Spielberg says that because the mechanical shark wouldn't operate properly on his film *Jaws*, it became a much better movie. If it had worked, they would've felt compelled to include a lot of shots of the robot shark going through the water, but, since they couldn't get the damn thing to look right, he had to come up with a work-around where they just used shots of the ocean and a cello playing. This adjustment made it much more scary by getting us to imagine the shark moving there below the surface, rather than if we'd seen the actual thing swimming around. And . . . if you haven't heard this fun fact: to write "crisis" in Chinese you use both the symbol for danger and the one for opportunity. Problems are messages. You get the idea.

JUST DO IT

While integrity and a sense of ownership about your contribution play a key part in meeting and mastering artistic challenges, you still need to allow for other interpretations and appreciate the massive transformations that can take place in postproduction. What I'm saying is that sometimes, as long as it's not too ghastly painful, it's best to just do the thing and trust that it will work out.

Trust plays a huge part in acting. Just as you have to trust yourself, you have to trust the talent of those you're working with. What's the alternative? Not to trust them? It's a matter of degree and subject to your specific situation, but, by and large, second guessing your collaborators takes a toll on your ability to wholeheartedly slip into the imaginary that is an unacceptable trade-off for whatever acts of bad taste or carelessness you can catch and remedy through your vigilance and calculation.

....

This stuff about trusting the artistry of your filmmakers does not apply, sadly, to either physical threats (stunts) or nudity. The enthusiastic and outright crazy people you encounter who create shows might be all too willing to risk your life, limb, and good name for the sake of a sensational shot. There are many, many stories of actors who've been gravely injured, and stories, lesser known perhaps, of modesties compromised. I worked with an actor on a movie who was sitting at the premier with her mother and father when she discovered that she had not, in fact, been framed just below the navel, as she'd been assured on the set, but well down the thigh of her totally nude body.

....

If you work for the camera you need to face the reality that, unless you get final cut (supremely rare for even the most successful actors), you simply can't be sure how your performance is going to be used in the final product. If you can't deal with that profundity, you better stick to acting for the stage. Good or bad, you can't possibly predict what the results of postproduction might create and you have little to no control over the way what you do in front of the camera gets used. They can take a reaction you had on one line and use it as a response to a different line. They can keep that camera running and use anything they catch you doing before "Action" and after "Cut." They can play with the image and sound and even get someone else to come in and dub your whole part if they want.

So, unless it's an extreme exception where you're really going to hate yourself, if you give up control and go for the quickest, easiest way to knock this thing out, it'll probably be OK.

Actors are continuously surprised by how, if they just go ahead and do a thing—make the move, say the line loud, or whatever the direction or necessity is—even if they don't beforehand feel they have a clear reason in their head for why they're doing it, it doesn't end up feeling so bad when they do it and no one notices anything weird in the final product. There will be times when what's asked of you seems absolutely and unquestionably repugnant and wrong, but usually the adjustment just feels vague and not fully motivated.

When this is the situation and you just do it mindlessly, there are several perfectly acceptable outcomes:

- You didn't understand how it was going to be used and it gets worked out in postproduction in some way, perhaps masked by something else or, when something is added, it makes sense.

- You do it and the audience, finding no sense to it, excludes it from their consciousness in favor of something in their experience that dominates.

- The audience actually invents and superimposes a value on this behavior consistent with their experience of the fictional context. While it's possible this might lead them off base, it is just as likely that they will fill it in with something good, I daresay possibly great (as was with the phenomenon where we projected great meaning upon the more or less blank ocean in *Jaws*).

• Your deeper talent fills the gap. Even if you don't feel a solid, imaginative connection to what's being asked of you, that's not to say your inventive genius isn't pulling it off beautifully. Maybe far better than your conscious plan.

STANDING YOUR GROUND

Now, having said all this about flexibility and being an adaptable pussycat, there is the hard truth that there may be battles to be fought and time you'll have to insist on taking or you don't deserve to call yourself an actor. All you really have to bring to the table is a core that channels the truth, and if you insult, corrupt, or starve that, then you're cutting yourself off from whatever it is you have to offer and you won't be any good to anyone, anyway.

I can't really advise you with much detail when it comes to the personality conflicts you're going to encounter while working, because each situation is so politically unique. I will recommend that before you make plain your willingness to go to war over a problem, you should be sure you've made yourself fully receptive to the input of others and—whether you like the personalities involved or not—fully examined each issue on its own merits.

In addition to confirmation bias corrupting your choices, you also have to deal with what's called "the backfire effect."

It's been documented that when people are shown plain evidence that what they believe is untrue, they tend to afterwards be even more entrenched in their positions.

Try to understand the spirit of the request without feeling you're being made a slave or a puppet and know that, when conflicts arise, more often than not the problem is a factor of clashing styles of communication. If you really feel dedicated to a certain way of doing something, there's still no value in aggravating a power struggle that might contaminate the project. I've explored this topic with many seasoned professionals and the prevailing recommendation for the course of action in these situations is feigned obliviousness.

That is to say, listen earnestly to the direction you know stinks to high heaven, nod with appreciation for the input, and then continue doing what you know is the right thing to do. If they bring up that you're not doing what was asked, act surprised that it didn't work out the way they wanted. Repeat if necessary. Adopt the position that when you're acting you're on automatic and aren't really responsible for what goes on when in this vacant state. You can get away with this because there actually are amateur practitioners of acting who are really like this. So, for now, you're one of those. Yes, it's dishonest and a bit degrading, but it's generally considered preferable to the ugliness of open warfare. Again, this is only to be used if the injury to your artistic integrity is genuine and great.

If outright head-to-head conflicts do arise, I offer that you needn't be unnecessarily dispirited. Such unpleasantness does not invariably damage the quality of your work. A lot of sub-par movies had wonderfully congenial film sets, while others, rife with ill will, nevertheless spawned masterpieces.

....

I consider Chinatown to be one of our greatest films and it had a notoriously stormy production. Among other incidents, there was one wherein director Roman Polanski destroyed Jack Nicholson's television by chucking it out the door of his trailer as he was watching a Lakers game. Polanski was apparently of the opinion that, regardless of it being a playoff, Nicholson should more properly be on the set.

....

IGNORE THE SIGHS

Even if it isn't a matter of direct conflict with someone in authority, you won't be immune to feeling pressure from the judgment of others who are watching you perform. Director David Lean spoke of a moment while directing *Lawrence Of Arabia* where there were five thousand extras in period costume staring at him as he was reflecting on his options. Maybe it won't be that many people eyeballing you as you're figuring out how to work out a new wrinkle, but there's a good chance you'll have somebody there with that look that says each minute you take is another clank of something coming out of the cash register.

But an actor is not a light bulb, and, regardless of how nice that would be for everybody, the process of executing something within a fiction is not the same as a mathematical problem that can be accomplished with direct, nose-to-the-grindstone application. It calls for delicate collaboration with inspiration . . . and inspiration doesn't care about your timetable. I tell directors they should treat actors the way they would an animal wrangler. The trainer will do his best to get the animal to give them what's desired, but he's dealing with a creature that operates with a different agenda. Your talent, like a bear or a crow or whatever, isn't especially bothered by the idea that failing to perform a trick perfectly will risk its opportunities for booking future work.

People don't get this. Even people who've worked on movies and television for years and who you'd think would know better. You may not see anyone actually rolling their eyes or moaning (although that's possible), but you will see them looking at each other and down at the ground and clearing their throats, and you'll sense the frustration from them that you're taking so long to work out your problem. They want you to get it done so that they can move on and feel themselves doing something useful. People don't get frustrated with the guy hammering a platform together. As long as he isn't holding a beer in one hand, they know he's taking the time necessary to do what he has to do. They understand that work. They don't understand yours.

Which is fine. You don't need sympathy for your creative struggles and you don't require their permission to do what you do. I'm not suggesting you be indulgently introspective or a dithering fool, and there's no excuse for not being fully prepared, but for those unforeseeable issues that you have to deal with on the day, no matter how agitated anyone gets about the time you take to do what you do, don't give one single damn about them. Make a deal you won't stand over their shoulders concerned with the pace of their work, and you can dismiss any opinions they have about the time it takes you to do yours. Be totally callous to any unrealistic annoyance anyone might have, secure in the knowledge that it is to their future benefit to have been involved with a project that contains quality work. Be clear I'm talking here about the demands of your creativity, *not comfort*. And don't you dare confuse the two.

Of course, the person you most have to worry about getting exasperated that the creative process isn't more mechanistic is yourself. If you're not careful, feelings of incompetence and shame about taking too much time will lead to your getting irritated and frustrated that something of genius isn't offering itself up immediately. And the truth is, all those looks and sounds you're reacting to probably have nothing to do with you at all. Those crew guys giving each other looks are doing it because no one noticed something they broke and fixed with tape. That guy staring at the ground is thinking about a recent mean remark he made. The moan you interpreted as someone's aggravation at you causing a delay is really that person realizing they forgot to return a phone call. Your ego is taking all these things as signs of persecution because it assumes everything that happens is some kind of reflection on itself.

GIVE YOURSELF A BREAK

If beating yourself up was effective in helping inspire you to devise and execute a new plan under pressure, I'd be all for it . . . but it isn't. Studies with pigeons, rats, monkeys, and human beings prove that encouragement with positive reinforcement works much better than harsh treatment when addressing creative challenges. The creative part of our natures, what's sometimes called "the right brain," is fed by greater blood flow in an environment low in punishment. If you want that worker chemical dopamine running high in your system, you have to give your ambitions a nice chunk of daylight to shoot for. Putting your focus on obstacles and fearing that a reprimanding whip is going to come down on you saps energy that would be better used exploring options and perfecting choices.

....

I feel compelled here to denounce a terrible, perverse methodology at play in the world. There are many who will tell you that if someone is especially bad and you punish them, they usually do better the next time, and if you praise someone who's done something especially well, the next time they won't do as well. The key word here is "especially." If someone is especially good or especially bad, then the next time they'll tend to be less like that, no matter how they've been treated. It is a phenomenon that applies to all statistics, including human behavior, called "regression toward the mean." The injurious scolding and potentially helpful praise withheld is reinforced by experiences following a law of the universe, things returning to the mid range, not—as it is misinterpreted— owing to this abusive practice.

....

If you allow the pressure to perform to over-stress you and become self-punishing, you're just going to gum up the system causing more delays, which will cause more frustration and put you in a terrible cycle. You might then latch on to some shoddy solution just to make the torture stop. Much better results will be had if you bathe the problem in optimism, humor, and gentle reassurance. Coax your feelings about the hurdle you face away from dread and toward thrill. Indulge in a little pride for what you do, and own that what really makes it special, the reason for the whole operation in the first place, the lights, the trucks, and so forth, is to bring forth and record that wild element, that beautiful, untamable art that's not supposed to be ordered around like a robot.

GETTING BETTER AT IT

There are different talents and different ways of nurturing them, but it's no secret that getting better at coping with pressure largely comes from experience. Steve Martin said that after so much public practice selling magic and entertaining at Knott's Berry Farm, he knew that when he went on a stage there was no way he wasn't going to be funny. Somebody who has that opinion of themselves, that's funny right there. How you personally go about getting performance exposure is up to you. You must produce like a producer produces. You can't be shy and you can't be humble. Not about this.

You have to do whatever you have to do to log those hours operating effectively under pressure and rack up a history of being able to depend on your acting techniques. The sooner you can get an audience response that's favorable, rather than demoralizing, the sooner you start building that self-perpetuating confidence. The validation that comes with repeatedly getting away with traipsing around pretending to be somebody else in public offers hope you can break through the pervasive stigma against acting and do it with less inhibition.

And don't kid yourself and think the cultural stigma against acting doesn't affect you. Oh sure, we put movie stars up on pedestals, but you've, nevertheless, gotten innumerable negative messages about showing off and being a glory hog or thinking you're so much better than everybody else that you deserve all the attention. Oliver Cromwell said, "Do not trust to the cheering, they would shout as much if you were going to be hanged." And conscious of it or not, you know this. You've seen the delight everyone takes in attacking those elevated movie stars if they dare make a slip. You know you're separating yourself from the crowd by being a performer, and so, at the merest hint, awareness of the risk you're taking can activate a deep fear response. You know if the tribe turns on you things can go very badly, very quickly.

The more experiences you acquire not being shamed for acting, the greater sense of ease and entitlement you'll develop about doing it. Of course, it's helpful if you had an upbringing where people praised the heck out of you every time you recited a poem or twirled around with your dress up over your head. Jodie Foster, in accepting her Oscar, probably rightly thanked her mother "for saying every picture I drew was a Picasso." But there are many performers, including Steve Martin, who overcame unsupportive families to make their show business aspirations real.

....

Increased experience will boost that valuable attribute of confidence, but after a certain point it won't, by itself, greatly improve your skills. If you want to get better at doing something, you have to constantly concentrate on the details of getting better at it. After you achieve a basic level of competence your system goes on automatic and your technique will tend to remain the same. Without the fear of failure, you function using your basic skills, or what's known as "bottom up" knowledge (unconscious), rather than "top down" knowledge (conscious). Apart from certain subtleties of trial-and-error growth, "good enough" rules the day and you plateau. This happens because we're all lazy.

Put another way, we are naturally wired to self-regulate and save exertions of will power (more on this in a moment) for times of real need. A hybrid car is designed to operate like this, using battery power whenever possible and only switching to gasoline when necessary. Unless you strive with a strong intention to override this automatic mechanism, you no longer affect how you're doing things and those areas remain fixed in their style of execution.

Developing skill into the elite level requires a continuous conscious effort to improve in the specific details of your work, and is significantly aided by having a qualified expert point out where greater application of this "top down" thought should be applied.

....

WELCOME FLOW

Everyone wants flow, or to be in what's called the "Zone" . . . to be unconsciously performing in a state of confident, energetic calmness where their skills are pouring out with perfect timing and amplitude. People with the talent for consistently achieving this condition of flow (who are called *autotelics*) are known for their curiosity, persistence, and for finding pleasure in being challenged by what they're doing at the moment, not for the sake of some later reward.

The Zone is frequently talked about in athletics, and it needs to be pointed out here, up front, that the experiences of flow and peak performance for someone in the arts is different from those in sports. Athletes have the luxury of ongoing measurable results to confirm the quality of their efforts, while an artist's work is largely subjective. Other than certain physical behaviors, like hitting your mark or putting a cup down at the right moment for continuity, an actor doesn't have concrete goals. And, especially in the sterilized environment of a recorded performance, they have little meaningful, real-time feedback for how what they're doing is being received. You can be operating at the height of your effectiveness and yet it may not seem all that wonderful at the time.

There's a story about a friend of Lawrence Olivier's going backstage after seeing him in a play that received a long, boisterous standing ovation and, that night, a particularly ecstatic response to Olivier's curtain call. He was prepared to heartily congratulate the actor, but when he entered the dressing room, all smiles, he found Olivier visibly upset, banging drawers and aggressively removing his costume. The shocked friend said to him, "Larry, the show was a great success. They loved you." To which Olivier replied, "Clearly. But I don't know why!"

It's possible to say that the worst thing about being an actor (apart from trying to make money from it) is that you can't tell how you're doing while you're doing it. You can feel great about your acting during a performance, all flushed with what you think is the appropriate emotion, and then, afterward, be disappointed by the assessment of trustworthy critics. Likewise, you can feel like you're doing terribly and just barely hanging on by your fingernails and afterward get a delighted response.

So, with this in mind, the bad news for you is you can never rest and you'll always be chasing a vague excellence that is constantly scooting away from you. The good news is that even if you think you're stinking up the place it might not be true and you can worry less about having that feeling.

Of course, without making your perceived sense of flow your measure of success (it is supposed to be about the audience having a good time, not you), it is nevertheless wise to practice the values that make it more likely you'll get closer to that special place of relaxed immersion and free expression. And for those times when you feel great about how it's going and then find out later you were right about how well it was going, well . . . that's why people are willing to ruin their lives to be actors.

CHOKE NOT

When flow is interrupted to the extreme it's called "choking" and it can happen to even accomplished experts. There are two types of choking, and either one can show up on the day. If you appreciate the threat and can spot the symptoms, you can take note of these unfavorable states as they start to come over you and move yourself back toward flow.

The most prevalent of these self-sabotaging mechanisms is when there's tremendous pressure to excel and you lose faith in your ability to perform. Having your confidence erode by itself is not the problem. As I said, as long as you keep your head in the game you can constantly doubt your skills and still be fine. But your fear can prompt you to make a radical change in your natural approach to your craft and cause you to become self-conscious and overly deliberate about executing individual behaviors. You go from doing what you do unconsciously (implicitly), to consciously attending to the details (explicitly). As your concentration darts about, recollecting, isolating, and trying to exert control, it switches on the wrong part of the brain, and, in the antithesis of flow, your performance crashes.

It's possible for this to happen as a result of the desire to do well alone, but it can also be triggered by the additional stress of being overloaded with directions you haven't had the chance to rehearse and habituate. The best safeguard for this is to have been fanatical in your rehearsal beforehand, ingraining every anticipatable element of your performance, so you've made sufficient room for what's not anticipatable on the day. Then, when acting, will yourself to project your focus on affecting the outside world, not your own functioning. Stay with what you're doing, your Action, and don't let your mind anticipate and visualize failure.

If you have the burden of performing behaviors you have not had an opportunity to habituate through rehearsal, execute each thing one at a time. Don't allow yourself to look too far down the road at the daunting mountain of details and imagine them overwhelming you. Trust that one part of your brain can do this work of execution while another, perhaps largely below the level of your awareness, is capable of engaging with the imaginary and rendering a totally believable performance.

The other type of jamming up happens when something alarming occurs out of the blue and you flip into panic mode. When something like this takes place you have the danger of either lunging for relief with poor execution or, more likely, going blank and flat-footed out of fear of making the wrong decision about what to do next. This kind of choking can get you physically hurt if it happens during a stunt, but as an actor you'll probably just botch what might have otherwise been an exciting take. The great director Sidney Lumet said that he would often do something startling during the audition process to see if the actor would stay in the scene or if they would lock up.

To prevent this condition you must, as with the other type of choking, refrain from thinking how awful it is that this is happening and restrain yourself from visualizing and connecting to the possibility of disaster ahead. You also need to commit to a technique that is absolute about the fact that neither lunging nor stalling is permissible, regardless of the situation. You have to have an essential grasp that reality is not going to alter its character because you get terrified and urgent, and you must be clear that in not making a decision, you've made one. Instill a certainty in yourself that the deer-in-the-headlights option is off the table and, no matter how lost you feel, percentages are going to be with your making an instinctive decision, even a reckless one, and staying with it.

The overall cure for choking and to return to flow is to remember to think when things go off the tracks: This is the adventure I'm supposed to be having, and, right now, I'm the lucky type.

AVOID "EGO DEPLETION"

Willpower, whether used to direct your concentration or deny gratification, is a resource like muscle strength that can be exhausted from continuous effort and requires replenishment to restore. This phenomenon, known as "ego depletion," is an issue to be aware of so you can nurture your mental acuity and make the best creative adaptations on the day.

Willpower is depleted by these factors:

- Holding focus on things not considered fun.

- Exercising impulse control (refraining from eating sugar, scratching an itch, etc.)

- Making choices (the more difficult and important, the more taxing).

- Maintaining a social front.

- Doing things thought deserving of a reward that go unrewarded.

- Feeling shamed.

- Low blood sugar, irritation, loneliness, and sleep deprivation (known in recovery circles as H.A.L.T., as in, "beware getting hungry, angry, lonely or tired.")

You should avoid too much of any of this stuff too soon before you get to the set. Make all foreseeable decisions, butter up all those who need buttering up (always a smart investment when opportune), and basically clear the decks of potential distractions so these issues aren't tapping energy you'll want available for your immediate work. By the same token, implementing a discipline for quieting your mind, a meditation, will help restore this asset.

There's a reason so many successful practitioners of their crafts settle on strict, solitary, pre-performance rituals. It frees them from the effort of making decisions and having to keep a social mask in place. It allows their willpower to rest and be at full capacity for their event. Having said this, not every performer has a ritual that involves solitude, because not everyone relates to socializing as work. This leads us to a very interesting aspect of ego depletion.

While this mechanism is still not fully understood, there does seem to be a connection between the supply of willpower and what each individual considers reward and punishment.

The power used to concentrate seems to be provided by a primitive aspect of our natures, the "id," and this aspect will deny its services unless it's refreshed by what it considers proper payment. To ward off exhaustion of the will, you can make deals with yourself by dangling rewards so that your psyche generates enthusiasm for the tasks it associates with resulting pleasures. Remember, though, these rewards are what your inner child considers a reward (praise, sugar, toys, fun, etc.), not what your better judgment deems worthwhile. Coming up with healthy ways to ply yourself to further the purposes of your better judgment can be challenging.

Apart from ego depletion impairing your ability to problem solve and be polite with others, both of which are necessary survival skills in the film and television business, there's also good, scientific evidence that being tapped out in this way inclines a person to be less empathetic. That's a serious problem. It's one thing to be prickly and unhelpful when issues need to be worked out on the set, but given compassion is a major component of good acting, now we're talking about messing with your actual performance. (My overall directive to actors is: Be a tuned-in, vulnerable egomaniac with *massive empathy*.)

Even when portraying a villain, you need empathy. Your character may not be swayed by it, they might actually take masochistic pleasure from it, but they still generate those internal pangs. As for playing a psychopath, please don't be fooled by movie versions of the condition that are rarely portrayed realistically with a total lack of empathy. If you are required to play that type, then you're job as an antagonist is, more or less, like that of the shark and you'll probably want to avoid playing this if possible because it's very two-dimensional and, as actual people, the void we sense in them makes them extremely dull. It's been called "the banality of evil."

The best overall tactic when it comes to dealing with ego depletion is application of the proper mindset. Test subjects coached to think of a task as drudgery described it as agony and quit much earlier than those primed to think of it as fun. Anyone who's raised kids knows this. The best way to handle children in many situations (and, remember, we're dealing with your child-self here) is to frame the work that has to be done as a game. With acting this shouldn't be that difficult. I mean, if you really look at it for more than two seconds, it's a pretty silly thing to call an occupation.

Everybody else on the set may be feeling under the gun and acting deadly serious, but that doesn't mean you should lose sight of how whacky it all is. On the other hand, working in an environment where people are intensely invested in their jobs is more fun than working some place where everyone's walking around like zombies, right? In dealing with my inner curmudgeon I find this quote very useful: "Even if the pessimist is right in the end, the optimist has a better time on the trip." By having a better time you'll likely increase your competence level, and you can invigorate your powers of concentration by maintaining a youthful sense of adventure.

BE HAPPY (IT LOOKS GOOD)

A character in the movie *Broadcast News* (written by James L. Brooks) has the line, "Wouldn't this be a great world if insecurity and desperation made us more attractive?" Well, it isn't that world, and it doesn't. Not only will the tension that comes with fear cause you to execute less effectively in creative situations, but there's an issue in acting of supreme importance that's different from most professions: looking good while you're doing it is part of the job.

The reason a dog puts its tail between its legs is to try and clamp down on the glands in its anus transmitting the smell of fear to other dogs (as opposed to wagging that confident smell around), and you, as you clamp down against your fear, not only are less available to do other things, but you telegraph it's not safe to be around you. In other words, it makes you repelling.

There are things you can do that will improve your internal chemistry and give you a more positive frame of mind. This may seem nutty (or obvious common knowledge by the time you read this), but we know that simply willing oneself to do certain behaviors will result in more good mood hormones (endorphins) and less stress/unhappy hormones (cortisol) in the bloodstream.

Feeling that you are faking these behaviors is totally fine and will nevertheless generate feelings that then make them seem less counterfeit and help perpetuate the process. Do whatever it takes to push through the stagnation that is often, in truth, a defensive crouch. Overcome the internalized voices of cynicism so you can get those juices flowing that will encourage conditions that are better for your work.

Things you can do that will give you a better attitude bump:

- Physicalize happiness.
  - Laughing and smiling.
  - Doing crazy/silly behaviors.
  - Dancing wildly.

- Recite positive affirmations.
  - "I am super powerful!"
  - "I am sexy as hell!"
  - "I love to be challenged!"

- Listen to happy or thrilling music.

- Visualize yourself in positive situations.
  - Being embraced with love.
  - In peaceful, soothing, or exotic surroundings.
  - Doing something heroic.

- Hold physical postures of confidence.
  - Stand with your feet spread wide and your arms outstretched as if you're having a big stretch.
  - Sit with your legs stuck far out and your hands clasped behind your head.
  - Stand with your feet planted wide and your fists placed proudly on your hips. This is called the "Wonder Woman."

YOUR EMOTIONAL PREPARATION

I'm not saying you should be skipping around, chipper as a cricket if you're in a fiction where your character is unhappy and frightened. I would never say that acting, whatever the nature of the part, should be fun. Joyous, yes, exhilarating, spirited, and gratifying, certainly . . . but not so trivial as to be called fun. In many cases, it's entirely appropriate to maintain a kind of darkness, keeping mostly to yourself and maintaining an interior life on quiet simmer. But I do believe you should, regardless of the emotional demands of the role, build your performance on a predisposition that where you work is a sunny place. Your acting context will produce deeper, more connected work if the foundation is an emotional state that is relaxed and secure.

There are schools of acting that advocate getting yourself into the same genuinely miserable condition as your character. Thinking themselves purists (and I was one for years), they hold the Truth of the character's situation is all that matters. But if you want to deal in Truth, the Truth is you're an actor choosing to put yourself into these fictional realities and that's undeniably a very different thing than living them in actuality. Do you really think you can get your deep psyche to go along with excluding that Truth? In my experience, actors tend to get deeper and do more effective work if, while still experiencing the emotions of fear, grief, and upset, they continue to connect to the joy of performing. It also reduces the wear and tear that risks limiting your output.

There's no question every artist who wants to claim themselves as one must have a willingness to appreciate the extremes of the human experience in their full agony. This can require going into very dark, personal places in your homework. There are certain conditions an actor will represent that cannot be achieved without a great deal of rough emotional preparation. In these situations it will probably be necessary to put yourself into contact with unhappy circumstances over and over in order to, in a manner of speaking, break yourself down.

All this can be done, however, while remaining within the reassuring bounds of fantasy and allowing for intervals of rest, and simultaneously experiencing the overall joy of creation and a sense of your mission: the inspiring of others. The pain, acute and crushing as it may at times be, does not need to be a continuous, self-inflicted torment that causes severe life disruption. Someone on a high wire can commit with more abandon if they know they're working with a net.

The confusion in this matter comes in part because we look at the many great artists who were unhappy and mistakenly think that if we were unhappy too it would improve our creativity. Oh, if only it were that easy. What you're probably seeing are people who've had major traumas, usually in early childhood, and, for whatever reason, they didn't adopt the normal coping mechanisms. And, so, without those filters, they suffer the brutalities of life more keenly and, yes, freely pour amazing stuff out into their art. Nevertheless, you won't get the same effect if you intentionally traumatize yourself because your psyche knows it's not a function of the tragedy of the human condition, it's just you being a jerk.

Whatever coping mechanisms you have, they are set on automatic, so overloading them with current unhappiness won't stop them from being operational and gumming up your output. By and large, that only aggravates them and creates distortions even worse for your art. What you have to do is—surgically and with all possible time and intensity—habituate removing those defense mechanisms while practicing the craft of acting, so you can then achieve better access to whatever deep stuff you've got.

There are indeed successful portrayals by actors willing to suffer continuously in the extreme for the sake of their acting, but I suggest this trauma has served a purpose probably better achieved through a different means. The value, if any, in self-inflicted torment is chiefly in its power as ritual, a pledge in blood the artist makes to their talent (and the Spirit?) that they will not shrink back from the fire on the day. This proof of one's conviction, however, need not be attained only through demonstrations of a willingness to damage one's life in sacrifice for a performance. It can be had with a simple, albeit profound, act of the heart.

Your entry into the imaginary ought to very much be taken on as a kind of sacred act, with an absolute commitment that, regardless of how disorienting or frightening what you encounter gets, the only way for you will be through it. You don't fight the rapids, you surrender and keep your head above water.

And do use ritual. Human beings respond deeply to them and you should develop rituals for each time you act and individualize them for specific roles. I'm simply suggesting, overall, that you seek to enjoy acting while you're acting because I believe celebrating your passion for playing pretend gives the audience a better experience. They are drawn to join with you in the ritual that is storytelling and you become more available to act as a vessel for that extra thing—call it what you will—inspiration, the Mystery, the Muse or, simply put, your talent.

Having said all this, it's really up to you. It's your private process and it's your life. If mortifying your flesh is what you have to do to get a great moment or two captured, well, so as long as it's your flesh and I'm getting to enjoy the show, have at it. If you want to stay in character and have people call you by your character's name, that's fine. You have to love Daniel Day Lewis who, when asked about his penchant for staying in character when he's working on a movie, said something to the affect, "I don't know that it makes my work any better, but it's fun and I can get away with doing it."

....

No one can tell you how to emotionally prepare. It might work for your instrument to recall actual events from your life, listen to evocative music, or look at a meaningful photograph or video. In my experience the most effective technique is for actors to daydream fictional events that generate "flashbulb memories" for their character. It's your personal business to pursue what works best for you and what is best suited for each role you do. I have recently, however, started to especially recommend the use of odors and sensations for their tremendous value in the area of emotional preparation, both within the fantasies you use to emotionalize yourself and in actuality.

People being monitored in an MRI scan were asked to consider a morally repugnant scenario and, while contemplating this, the same part of their brains activated as if something rotten was being smelled. The same thing happens with other scenarios and primitive parts of the brain devoted to specific odors, tastes, and sensations.

Tests have shown that if someone asks you to hold a warm object, as opposed to a cold object, you will later tend to consider that person as friendlier. You think of them as a "warmer" person. There is a direct correlation with how we use many words, such as "chilling," "sweet," "disgusting," or "bitter," and the emotions they describe. Unlike with information we receive through our hearing or sight that is routed through the higher brain functions and is subject to being censored, stimuli from odors, tastes, and skin sensations go directly to the deep, emotional part of the brain (the amygdalae).

The technique I'm suggesting is to expose yourself to a particular odor/taste/sensation prior to your first moment that is consistent with how you want to feel: sweet and warm for being kindly disposed, sour or cold for repelled or frightened, bitter and foul for alienated or disgusted, and so forth. Exposure to these vivid stimuli can be used in preparation to create pre-set, Pavlovian responses. If there's a circumstance that occurs during the scene where you'd like a vivid response, run the scene in your imagination (or rehearsal if you have an indulgent partner) and then, when you get to that moment where the given event occurs, bite into a warm brownie, sip some pure lime juice or take a sniff from a jar of something particularly awful. Use whatever makes sense for the reaction you want in the scene. Instruct someone to pour ice water down your back at the appearance of the vampire.

....

YOUR KILLER INSTINCT

For an actor, for any artist who must perform on command, the talent required for being effective during times of expectation is primary. The very aspect of something that is planned meeting the unpredictable in a charged atmosphere makes it what it is. The particular genius for this is what I call "Killer

Instinct," and there are individuals who excel at nothing so much as their ability to get more focused under stress and allow their deep talent for effectiveness to come through. In sports these people are called "money players."

Boxing coach Cuss D'Amato said, "Everybody's got a plan 'til they get hit in the mouth." And all the preparation—the choices, the hours you've rehearsed, the lines, the blocking, the emotional preparation, the rhythms and the beats and the nuances you have in mind—doesn't mean squat if you can't make it come off on the day.

Those with Killer Instinct may have less fear because their basic biology produces less fear, or it may be because they relate to the task as less frightening, whether out of a deep faith in their own competence or because they just don't see a lot of downside to failure. It's possible, on the other hand, that someone enjoys what might be thought of as a pure Killer Instinct and, while just as scared as anybody else, they're able to isolate and lock down on what's key without allowing for any second guessing. In this way, they use their fear to do good work, understanding it's all on them to perform and no one is going to come to the rescue because they act like a needy mess.

This talent is related to the basic survival mechanism in all living things and there are just certain individuals in whom it is more expressed and certain situations that tend to bring it out. You want to have acting be one of the things that brings it out of you. You must get clear about your relatedness to performing and engage the can-do spirit, a sacred commitment that the show must go on. In this way you can harness the same primal power utilized by other challenging professions, such as emergency care workers or members of the military's special forces.

This is what actors are using when they lose scary amounts of weight for a part or volunteer to do intense action sequences instead of requesting stunt doubles. Actors go on stage regardless of raging fevers with the audience never guessing they're anything but fit. If people connect to a sense of mission and allow for no alternative, they can endure tremendous hardships without experiencing the discomforts nearly as distractingly fearful as when there's an expectation of coziness.

One of the most amazing statistics in sports is the number of long-distance running records held by people who come from one tribe in Kenya—the Kalenjin. The best explanation for this seems to be that, way beyond the physical aptitude these people have for running, they're trained from a very early age to endure extreme pain. It's done with both boys and girls in preparation for a torturous initiation ritual they undergo that is crucial to their resultant stature in life. Long-distance running is very painful and these Kenyans are conditioned to relate to pain differently.

The best thing an actor can do to deal with the stresses that will undoubtedly arise when called to perform under challenging circumstances is to relate to these stresses as less abhorrent. Those stage nerves flooding you with dread are misrepresenting what's going on and that sense of jumpy fragility is wrong when it tells you you're out of your element. Our normal, civilized lives are so full of luxury that our gauge for discomfort gets very sensitized . . . some would say out of whack.

Maybe you've had the experience of feeling a desperate need to go to the bathroom or felt an urgency to eat and then lost that feeling for some reason, even though your bladder was just as full or your stomach just as empty. You felt the impulses, you just didn't have the same frantic urge to fix the situation. This demonstrates how your sensitivity to stimulation is relative. You can take greater command over these impulses if you know this about your internal mechanisms and counter them with the tremendous life force that comes from having a sense of purpose.

A defining feature of life is that it is an organized thing adapting to the hardship of conditions that are working to make it disorganized. Facing unpredictable challenges is what you're built for and executing under pressure is a natural phenomenon that all life is designed to do, not something outlandish. There's nothing wrong with a little good discomfort.

WANTING IT THE RIGHT WAY

Employing your Killer Instinct as it relates to your passion to perform is tricky, because it's not necessarily the one with the greatest desire who achieves the greatest access to this talent. There's a paradox. While you do want to sustain an intense drive for making what you do great, at the same time it's probably best if you don't care that much about how great it is while you're doing it. You will see performers with seemingly little investment in their work do better than those far more earnest because they have less at stake and carry themselves with an attractive looseness. This is the gift of flexibility and self-perpetuating confidence observable in established stars who, knowing they've got three more jobs lined up after this one, easily swagger up to their mark.

An actor may want very, very much to do well because doing well means they might get more opportunities to act, get validation as an artist, and acquire more money and comfort, but the wanting of these things is not the final word on the matter. Your talent is, and ever will be, a wild creature that doesn't bow down to those objectives, and it might just say, "to hell with all this desperate pressure," and leave you on your own. Then, when you sense the absence of these rich elements, you might start to panic, generating more stress and fear, and go into a self-perpetuating cycle of insecurity.

If you're going to resolve difficulties and rise to your best on the day, you may have to face some thorny, psychological issues. It's possible the impulse that brought you into acting will be the greatest obstacle to your acting. Maybe you're acting so you can get some glory because someone from your past pushed you into the background, giving you the message it wasn't safe to stand out. Maybe you want to express feelings you suppressed because you were taught those feelings, if revealed, would make you less loveable. Maybe you took on playing pretend to compensate for some lack in your life and you can't help begrudging the necessity for this compensation, like an amputee hating their prosthetic leg and wanting to hurl it across the room.

The idea of completely laying it all out there and actually doing your absolute best is frightening. If, for instance, you did allow yourself to fully apply your skills and imagination and the result was less than your ascent into legend with comparisons to Brando and Streep, you might be gravely disappointed. If you gave away all control over how you were going to be received and truly aspired to something big and were then snubbed by the crowd, you might imagine it worse than having purposefully orchestrated a failure. Walking away with the sense of being a loser may be crappy, but it is familiar. Everyone knows that feeling very well.

You might prefer a lot of very unpleasant outcomes rather than knowing you rendered the best possible acting you could ever bring to bear and gave your best shot at getting the objective that brought you into acting, but, even so, were still unable to fix the past. This would mean you would be forced to face the fact that nothing you could achieve through acting was ever going to improve your mom's nurturing abilities, or keep your dad from walking out, or be able to expunge the family grief.

BE WILLING TO SUCCEED

Besides the fear of giving your best efforts and meeting with failure and disappointment, you might not do as well as you possibly could so you can avoid the results of success. If you became transported and really embodied strength or sexuality or vulnerability, you might have to take responsibility for owning such characteristics and that would mean change. This is what Abraham Maslow called the "Jonah Complex," named for the biblical Jonah who resisted God's command to take His message into the world.

There's been a lot of writing on the subject by great authors through the centuries, as well as a lot of recent literature using the paradigm of "abundance mentality," so I won't dwell on the point here. But it is, without question, something you should consider as it pertains to the larger perspective of your life and how it can create inhibitions on the day.

The Jonah Complex can be identified by these fears:

- Fear of being prominent or having authority because it challenges your self image.

- Fear of the responsibility that comes with power.

- Fear that having an extraordinary life will be alienating to others.

- Fear of being seen as arrogant, self-centered, etc.

- Fear that entering new situations will create disorientation, reveal incompetence, and attract unwanted attention.

- Fear of the pain when success is inevitably taken from you.

When acting on camera the environment is such that you probably won't be receiving a great deal of open, positive reinforcement for your acting and you must guard against filling this vacuum with projections of your Jonah Complex, interpreting the lack of cheers for disapproval. Film crews operate with the understanding they are there to facilitate the capturing of your performance, not to function as an audience themselves. This context is firmly reinforced by the need for absolute silence while you're acting. Therefore, you must, along with the fictional world you create, imagine those open-hearted, supportive souls for whom you're acting.

Even after "Cut!" is called, you have to accept that film crews aren't necessarily composed of the most gregarious personalities who are given to open expressions of enthusiasm. The world of their jobs is where something either gets done or it doesn't get done, and gradients of subjective value are rarely part of their work. No one pats the assistant cameraman on the back and says, "That was wonderful how you put on the correct lens."

With everyone properly associating great importance to your job as an artist, and with what is likely near total ignorance on their part about the actual process of acting itself, the crew you're working with might appear standoffish as they try not to disturb whatever the hell it is you're doing. They may not feel free to voice encouragement for your work for fear your response might be something like, "How dare you insult me by acting surprised I could do this well." Or simply, "I don't need your approval."

Regardless, you must not let anyone's behavior in the environment undermine your confidence with thoughts you're being arrogant or a "fancy pants," and you certainly shouldn't misinterpret their reserve for negative judgment. Of course everyone present wants you to do great and become a star because of a show they've worked on. Your success could only be a good thing for them.

Marianne Williamson said, "Your playing small does not serve the world." And, while your older sister may have given you that impression, it didn't actually serve her either. Be willing to step out into no man's land where new things—like big-time success—will challenge you and make you grow in new ways. Risk getting deep, getting wild, getting ugly, and getting what you want.

CARE AND DON'T CARE

Your best approach on the day will probably be to burn with a desire to do well and do everything possible to ensure that that happens, but when the time comes, at some point before you walk to the set, surrender it all up and don't really care that much about the final results. Let the heavy stuff fall away, think less, worry less, and start believing today is your lucky day. As much as you hunger to be great, apply that to the strategy of not wanting it so much. Embrace the paradox.

The basketball player Robert "Big Shot Rob" Horry was legendary for making hugely important clutch shots at the end of championship games. He would celebrate in exaltation with the rest of his team over the wins he created, but when asked his secret for possessing such icy calm during these incredibly intense moments, he responded by saying, "I have a very sick daughter so I think I have a pretty good sense of proportion about the game." Since his retirement, Robert Horry's daughter died from her genetic disorder at age seventeen. So, yeah, maybe keeping a good sense of proportion would help.

An audience's willingness to offer their time and open hearts to you is a huge gift, and you may experience this as a problem. If you received an extravagant gift from a stranger, you'd feel uneasy about it and either insist on giving it back or resent your inability to restore the balance. But, what if the giver wasn't a stranger? In the book of Matthew it's written that to get into heaven you must "become like a child." I think an actor might be served in relating to the camera this way. Be a child. Vulnerable and innocent, truly, but, also like a child, know you require love and fully expect to get it. This can be your agreement with the audience.

YOU'RE ALWAYS WHERE YOU SHOULD BE

While there may be tremendous problems on the set with unforeseen, difficult, and agonizing adjustments, there's another possibility, as well: Magic. From the earliest age of mankind it's been known there's a special connection between the real world and the one created through art. There are portals made available through means we don't fully understand, but which are related to a reverence for a sense of occasion.

What happens on the day is the crucible and the raison d'être for everything you're supposed to be about as a performing artist. It isn't about the talk and the getting ready and then, later, the celebrating and the talk. It is about doing it. Actually doing it. After all the adjustments and under all the pressure, it's nevertheless your job to make it look easy and effortless and as if you're totally in your element. As if there's no place you'd rather be.

Being wedded to that sensibility that there's no place you'd rather be, you put yourself closer to the elemental, animal state we want in our performers. Animals know and live what we humans must be told by our wisest thinkers, such as Alexander Pope who stated at the end of his poem *An Essay On Man*, "Whatever is, is right." In this way, animals carry themselves, as any fine actor does, with the quality that their whole lives have been leading them to this very moment.

When you act, separate yourself from the rules we commonly live by in our civilized world. Meet your obligations to execute all the necessary technical requirements, but free yourself from all societal obligations and judgments. You must seek maximum effectiveness while still fully experiencing the emotions consistent with the magnitude of the imaginary circumstances. Dissociating and compartmentalizing (so rewarded in our culture) is a cheat that actors are not allowed. When you're acting, leave yourself alone. Take a break from trying to fix everybody. Take off the mask, take off the chains (they're probably not even there anymore), get something you can believe in and be a channel for it.

It may take some private work, perhaps some form of therapy, to clear away the blockage that's preventing you from sharing the full scope of your gifts. You should surround yourself with positive people. And, again, practice, practice, practice. Your talent wants to come out. Find some trustworthy guidance and acquire good acting techniques, then get in front of an audience, feel the pressure, feel the imaginative world beckoning and do your thing.

A camera should be thought of as the perfect receiving and sharing presence, always there, where and when it should be. There's no point in pretending it isn't catching everything, and everything it's catching is what ought to be caught. You can dazzle like the biggest blaze in the universe or connect to the smallest next-to-nothing there is. It's impossible to be too much or too little. It's all fine.

Everything is a version of Truth and yours is to work for a simpler, more clear version.

THE INTERVIEWS

....

Following are interviews with seasoned film professionals; some my oldest and dearest friends, including former students, others more recent relationships, and some I only know through mutual acquaintance. Done in either L.A. or New York, a few of these exchanges took place in restaurants, others in living rooms, and several on the phone (I spoke with Michael Rymer on a lengthy drive he had to a location in Australia). All gave their time upon being asked largely out of a love for the art and a desire to see it flourish.

Although the interviewees have interesting and instructive careers, there's little biographical information included. My aim is to cut to the heart of what specifically makes you excellent on camera, and, in addition to that excellence, what makes people want to work with you again. The advice here includes invaluable insider observations, and, while a wide range of perspectives is offered, there is a strong, common thread: the power of authenticity.

To commit one's life, as these people have, to the art of cinema is a reckless and noble thing. Reckless because it is extremely unpredictable as a career, and, in practice, a kind of answering to "the call of the void" (that irrational impulse one has to jump from a great height or into dark water, or to eat the whole pie). Noble because they go into that void, for us all, in search of meaning to the fantastic and terrible realities of existence.

I learned a great deal from these conversations. I think you will, too.

. . . .

PETER BOGDANOVICH INTERVIEW

Director (*The Last Picture Show; Paper Moon; What's Up, Doc?*), writer, actor, producer, essayist.

D.W. Brown: What would you say it is that makes a film performance effective?

Peter Bogdanovich: I think the most effective movie performances are those where the line between the actor and the character is erased. There should be no sense of it being a character, but rather a real person.

D.W. Brown: When James Cagney was asked what's most important in acting he said, "Don't get caught doing it."

Peter Bogdanovich: That's right. You find the character in yourself.

D.W. Brown: You've worked in a lot of different styles. What would you suggest to an actor about playing the difference between, say, realistic drama and screwball comedy?

Peter Bogdanovich: When you're doing comedy, generally you should go quickly. You want to pick up the pace. Let it go by fast. You have to be believable, but you also have to speed up. You have to find the style that the screenplay and the director are taking you toward. If it's a screwball comedy, that's one thing, and, if it's a drama, that's another thing. If it's a western, that's different than a crime picture. Everything has a different style and a different tempo. The thing is you need to be believable in whatever you're doing. Be real. Find ways to make things happen faster, if that's what you have to do because it's a comedy, but that doesn't mean you're not focused within each moment. Just, sometimes you have to go faster.

D.W. Brown: How would you address that old question of what you should do if someone is giving you a direction you disagree with?

Peter Bogdanovich: Well, that is a difficult situation.

D.W. Brown: Yes, and I know it's hard to speak to this because these situations usually have unique political and psychological components all their own.

Peter Bogdanovich: If you don't think what the director is telling you is right, just tell him OK and do whatever you want. Tell him you understand what he means, and then do what you want, and by and large he might think that's exactly what he wanted. A lot of times the director doesn't know what he wants. He won't know until he sees it.

D.W. Brown: Right.

Peter Bogdanovich: That's why they ask actors to do it again and often don't even give direction. They just say, "Do it again?" because they hope that, this time, it'll be right. They don't know what they want, because they haven't heard it yet.

D.W. Brown: Or if they do have a vision of it, they don't know how to address it to an actor. They'll talk about it in intellectual terms, which usually doesn't help anybody.

Peter Bogdanovich: An actor really needs to know what's required without the help of a director. You can't count on the director. You just can't. Often times the director doesn't help you at all.

D.W. Brown: I've started telling my students that they need to think about themselves the same way the electrician does. Nobody understands what you're doing and they don't want to talk to you. Then, if they encounter a director who knows how to talk to actors, they can be pleasantly surprised.

Peter Bogdanovich: That's a good way of putting it.

D.W. Brown: With television and even a lot of high-budget filmmaking now the schedules are so tight, what kind of advice can you give an actor when they want to do quality work, but they're facing this constant pressure to move on?

Peter Bogdanovich: Well, it's true, a lot of times now a director will say you've got one or two takes and that's it, so you have to be ready to give it to them on the first take. You don't know how many you're going to get.

D.W. Brown: Would you caution actors to be careful not to try to do too much with a part, and to keep it simple and economical, because there just isn't going to be the time to explore a lot of possibilities?

Peter Bogdanovich: I think you have to hone it down to the best ideas rather than going off in too many different directions, but I think it's always good to have a lot of ideas. If the director doesn't like it he can always tell you not to do that. But I think it's always worth bringing in as much as you can.

D.W. Brown: How much do you think an actor should concern themselves with continuity?

Peter Bogdanovich: Well, you've got a script supervisor to help you with that, but I think it's important. If it's a scene that requires a lot of business, you ought to plan out and get comfortable with the business before you do it. Get very comfortable with the business. If you're cooking a meal and you have dialogue, you better work on that for a while. Get to know the business, get it out of the way so it's second nature. You won't have time to work on that on the set, so you have to practice that at home.

D.W. Brown: How about matching in terms of emotional tones? You'll hear different opinions on this. Some will say if you don't peak in the same place in a given scene, you're hurting yourself. Others will say you shouldn't have your attention on that, and that you should, more or less, just let it rip.

Peter Bogdanovich: I think it is a question of making everything fresh each time. The camera captures freshness. If it seems rehearsed and polished, it's not going to read right. It should feel like what John Ford called the "first time emotion."

D.W. Brown: What traps do you see actors fall into?

Peter Bogdanovich: An actor should pay as little attention to the camera as possible, because he doesn't know what to do with it, and it's not going to help him to know it. Forget it.

D.W. Brown: Don't worry about your coverage.

Peter Bogdanovich: You can't start thinking about that. That's none of your business. That's the director's job. Know your words and have a sense of how you want to play the scene. Then listen to the other actor and play off of them.

. . . .

CATHERINE HARDWICKE INTERVIEW
Director (*Thirteen, Twilight, Lords of Dogtown*), writer, producer, production designer.

D.W. Brown: I know a lot of sets are pretty hectic places and don't feel like very creative environments. What would you say to an actor who has to come onto the set and get in flow?

Catherine Hardwicke: Oh, I have some days that are absolute disasters. Everything goes wrong and you're way behind. So, how a person can find their own center in that can be very difficult. That's the challenge, you know. And we have to try to find that, all of us. Try to leave the stress outside, avoid the stresses. Maybe do visualizations. Some way to try to get back to a good place.

D.W. Brown: An actor has to allow for all kinds of things where they're trusting in the filmmakers, don't you think?

Catherine Hardwicke: Absolutely. Maybe the actor will do something that isn't consistent with the arc of the character and the editor has to remove it. I've had situations where the actor will get too emotional, where there's too much emotion and it has to be pulled back at that point in the scene. The actor may feel very honest, that they're being very truthful, but it's too much at that point in the story. That character may have many more scenes they have to get through.

D.W. Brown: I think performers may be prone to having that situation because they come into acting for the very reason that it's a place to get out their feelings. So, when they feel those feelings, there can be this, "Ah ha! I'm doing what I'm supposed to be doing."

Catherine Hardwicke: Yes. But we don't necessarily want to see somebody just crying, crying, crying.

D.W. Brown: How conscious do you think an actor should be about continuity?

Catherine Hardwicke: There are two sides to that. An actor should have the freedom, but on the other hand if we're doing a long scene and the glass keeps changing hands we're going to have a problem. You do have to sometimes sacrifice moments that you love because the continuity would be just too outrageous. But still, I really do not want the script supervisor to be, you know, crazy pointing out every single little thing. I'd rather the actor be fully in it.

D.W. Brown: Heath Ledger was such an amazing actor and you worked with him making *Lords of Dogtown*. What was your experience with him like?

Catherine Hardwicke: He was very excited about playing the part. And then, at a certain point, he decided he couldn't do it and said he was going to have to back out. His insecurity level spiked. Then he came back and said, OK, I'm in. Then he came to the little monkey rehearsal I had at my house and he was very embarrassed, very shy about showing what he was doing. The thing about him was that when he finally did surrender himself, he went into an entire body thing, you know, he was very physical. He became this very loose, wild surfer kind of guy. He had teeth made that matched the guy. He thought that that would help in getting to the character. He did his hair this wild way. He slowly built up this very full feeling for the character and his entire body language became that loose way and it was very special and six days later he was shooting *Brokeback Mountain*, six days after he finished ours and he had an entirely different physicality and his voice was completely different. And he only had six days to do it. I know because he was on my set six days before that. It just blew my mind that he could make such a physical transformation. And I think being grounded in your body is a great, beautiful lesson there. Your body movement, what that can tell you. I see a lot of actors who don't have that. He was also very creative every minute on the set. He was very encouraging of all the younger actors. He would be very unpredictable and the way he would do things it would be like, 'I'm just going to try this.' A lot of the things he did were unpredictable and even a little scary. Almost dangerous. But alive, just so alive.

D.W. Brown: Maybe that in part explains his initial fear. He knew that once he got to the edge of the cliff, if he jumped, he was all in and there was no going back.

Catherine Hardwicke: Yeah, I think so. He was such a mysterious person in so many ways.

D.W. Brown: How do you help the actors get a feel for the style you're going to be going for?

Catherine Hardwicke: I'll try to establish that in the rehearsal.

If it's a very small part and they haven't had a chance to be part of the rehearsal process, I try to do it in the audition itself. For me, during the audition, if an actor can hear what the director is saying and can make it their own, an internal, personal adjustment, it makes a huge difference because then I know they can take the note and make something beautiful and individual out of it, not just take a note on the nose and literal. If they just can't take an adjustment in a fluid way, or they can't take it at all, then they're not coming back.

D.W. Brown: I can understand that, because it's scary to imagine that they would be there on the day with you and they get locked up.

Catherine Hardwicke: That's right, and why would I want to have that person there when there are so many talented actors who can do the work. They can take the note and find some way of incorporating it and feel it for themselves. I really believe the best kind of training is improv training. It's really even the best thing for writing, the best thing for pitching, everything really, life.

. . . .
JON GRIES INTERVIEW
Director, actor (*Napoleon Dynamite, Taken, Will Penny*).

D.W. Brown: What do you think the distinctions are between stage and film acting?

Jon Gries: I would say the first thing is that because on stage you're running the continuum of your performance all the way from the beginning to the end, there are obvious technical differences. Stage is more language oriented, whereas the cinema is a visual medium. Having the opportunity to live the life of the character you're playing from the beginning to the end at the curtain is much more organic than shooting a fight with your mother in one room and then stepping into another room and maybe not acting that scene, which will appear as if happening a half second later, until maybe weeks later, or maybe you've shot it weeks earlier.

D.W. Brown: What do you think makes a film performance effective?

Jon Gries: You try and find those moments. Sometimes I think in terms of music. I think in terms of the beat. The actual beat. You know, Paul Newman said he tried to throw the beat off a little bit, but still keep it in the measure. I think that's pretty much what I'm trying to find, especially in close up. Feeling the beat, but working between those beats.

D.W. Brown: Like syncopation.

Jon Gries: Yeah. You can come early with an idea, maybe before something is actually revealed. Maybe your character can have a moment not understood by them fully, but where they're ahead and figuring it out before it's actually proven. They may have a dawning ah-ha moment even before the evidence has been presented to them. And it's a personal, private thing. An intuitive anticipation. I certainly don't mean the bad kind of anticipation where you brace before getting sucker punched. It's your job to hide the fact that that kind of shock is coming. I don't want to say anticipating in the sense of being not surprised. But there are times when there can be perhaps anticipating in the sense of having a gut feeling that this moment is primed.

D.W. Brown: That's really interesting, because that moment of emotional impact is so important with film, then, if your character has some kind of prescience, I don't know, they had a dream about it, but a kind of deep sense that this event was somehow in the cards. Then when it happens you can really have it come crashing in. Surprised, yes, because everything in the moment is surprising, but your worst fear realized or the greatest thing possible you secretly dared to hope for now getting confirmed. Boom, it goes right to your center.

Jon Gries: Yes. It's a different choice than when you're surprised out of the blue and had no clue something like this could happen. But it doesn't have to be any less impactful to have it be a kind of "damn, I knew it."

D.W. Brown: There's a lot of recorded material that will get used in a movie in a way that an actor can't predict. Do you have any awareness of this reality during filming?

Jon Gries: There are some directors, and I personally love those kind of directors and I try and emulate that kind of director when I direct personally, who are very much about capturing what's going to happen around the scene's dialogue, before and after what's written down. Whenever what's written is done you can watch actors and feel their anticipation of the director saying, "Cut." I tell myself never, never cut the scene in your mind. Keep playing it all the way through. Even to the extent that if you hear "Cut," stay with it. Especially now in the digital age, where they may say "Cut," and right away go back to one and they just keep running the video. You want to stay in it, absolutely.

D.W. Brown: How about style, which is so tough to nail down. What's your best advice for how to get a feel for the style of what the presentation is going to be?

Jon Gries: This is actually a great question. When, as an actor, I come onto a film and I'm going to go to the location somewhere, invariably they'll say, "All right, your start date is on the twenty-fifth, so we'll fly you out on the twenty-third and you can do your costume and get situated one day before and then shoot the next day." I'll say I'd like to be there on the twenty-first, or the nineteenth, even, so I can spend a couple days on the set watching. Just watching how this film is being shot. It can totally impact my choices. I want to see what's being done because sometimes directors can't explain it in a way where you can get a feel for it. Sometimes all I need is ten minutes just watching the monitor. Watching what the approach is.

. . . .

MICHAEL RYMER INTERVIEW

Director (*Battlestar Galactica*, Emmy nomination; *Queen of the Damned; Angel Baby*), writer, producer.

D.W. Brown: What makes someone effective on screen?

Michael Rymer: I would say that the most basic thing is to be excited by someone. If they bring the text to life. This is not always obvious. Perhaps a character is set up a certain way, but, specific to the role, you're looking for someone who can play around the notes. If it's a soft character, you might want someone who can bring a little edge to it. If it's a very strong person, you want someone who can show some vulnerability through that. You want an actor who has some dimensions. I guess in the audition I'm, in part, looking for an actor's process. A lot of actors come in and can do a good audition, but then, on the set, that's all you ever get. You always want to keep the process continuous, to have more development and more progression to it. You want to get to the bottom and to the edges of the scene and the material. You don't want it dead on arrival.

D.W. Brown: On the other hand, you know the incredible time crunch happening with many projects. What can you say to an actor who feels that pressure of the clock ticking, but still wants to express something special?

Michael Rymer: To me, if I was looking for the common quality amongst really good actors, the excellent actors, it begins with a sense of entitlement. That works on many levels. One is that they believe that, as an actor and a character, they have enough to hold your attention. And that also applies to the understanding that, while you do have to do it quickly and only have so many takes, you have to make sure you leave the psychological space for yourself to do your best stuff. You can't be rushed and panicked and out of body and not in the moment.

D.W. Brown: When I talk to actors about this, I'll tell them that, in the same way a cinematographer can't rush their work so it's out of focus and unusable, an actor has to take the time they need to do a proper job, or they aren't really fulfilling their obligation. Although, it's easy to talk about all this, but, as you know, when you're actually in some of these environments it can be very, very pressurized and those great intentions can go out the window.

Michael Rymer: It's an extremely difficult environment at times to be fully present and fully able to bring your best stuff. I guess that's true of many professions really, whether it's an athlete or a chef, you could be the calmest person in the world, but you have to deliver under pressure and that's it. There's no substitute for experience, of course. The more you've done and the more you been through it, having the experience of TV where it's very often rushed. It's your fluidity that enables you to get to that place where you have that confidence. Even if you're nervous and feeling the pressure you have enough experience to know that you can get it out and that causes you to relax. Having said all this about experience, though, still, that youthful thing can burn very brightly in a beautiful way.

D.W. Brown: Oh, no doubt. And an actor being economical in the way they use themselves can become a canned, airless performance.

Michael Rymer: Absolutely. There's actually a whole other skill that I'm just starting to grasp. Watching how these experienced actors do things, like they'll take their glasses off or take a sip of the glass and they're very specific about where they do it. And it occurred to me not too long ago that in doing it in that way they were forcing the cut. They know we have to show them doing this bit of business otherwise the continuity will be off with the cup going in and out of their hands, but they pick the spot in the scene they think is the key moment that needs to be on camera and that's where they put their little arabesque in order to make sure that this particular footage is used. And, by the way, I don't think there's necessarily anything wrong with it.

....

WILLIAM MAPOTHER INTERVIEW
Actor (*Another Earth, Born on the Fourth of July, Mission Impossible II*).

D.W. Brown: What are the most important factors of an effective performance on camera?

William Mapother: Relaxation. Being present in the moment. Intention. Being absolutely truthful, because the audience is not in the back of a large theater, but right in front of you as the camera and the mike.

D.W. Brown: What kinds of things hurt a performance on camera?

William Mapother: Pushing. Faking. The camera is so close and sees everything.

D.W. Brown: Can you speak to the ways in which an actor should consider and be influenced by the editor's job with respect to their performance.

William Mapother: This is a complicated issue with several aspects. For one thing, if the editor is good, you can trust him. Unfortunately, it's usually tough for an actor to know if an editor is good, unless you know his previous work, because actors usually don't see an editor's work until after shooting is completed. And sometimes it doesn't even help if the editor is good, because even a good editor might not, or can't, choose an actor's best take because of other issues. For example, it was a bad take for the camera, or a line was done improperly by another actor in your two shot. If an actor limits the variety of his performance because he fears an editor will pick a bad take, he's also potentially limiting his own ability to react in the moment, because he's keeping watch over himself. Not trusting the editor usually also means that the actor isn't trusting the director, because he usually supervises and approves the editor's work. So, restricting the variety of choices the editor receives means restricting the choices the director receives, which can mean refusing to take direction while shooting and all the implications that has. In general, I try to give a wide a variety of takes, but all within the character's ballpark. This allows the editor and director the best opportunity to craft my character's arc over the movie. That freedom is important in postproduction, because of unforeseeable circumstances. For instance, an entire scene is cut, which means they have to compensate with material from other scenes. I've learned to accept that it's part of the filmmaking process and the actor influences only a small slice of that process. I came to that acceptance after an experience on the TV show *Lost*. My character Ethan had been kicking everyone's butt, and we were shooting the episode in which Ethan is beaten up by Jack, then shot and killed. In order to justify how Jack could beat him, we shot a scene in which Ethan first gets stabbed in the leg and wounded. So, when we see Ethan later in the episode, of course I played it with a limp. No problem, right? Well, in postproduction they cut the knife-in-the-leg scene, so when we see the kind of super-human Ethan in the jungle, he's limping for no reason, as if he twisted his super-human ankle on a root or something. That's when I really came to accept the limitations of our best efforts.

. . . .

PETER MACNICOL INTERVIEW

Actor, (*Ally McBeal*, Emmy Outstanding Supporting Actor; *Sophie's Choice; Battleship*) director, writer.

D.W. Brown: How much should an actor be influenced by the job of the editor in their performance?

Peter MacNicol: Well, helping the editor is helping yourself. You want the cutter to have the highest number of good takes on you as possible. If you limit the editor's choices, by mismatching your actions or not syncing up emotionally from one size to another, then you harm yourself. They will have to cut around what might have been your best take or best moment within a take because you sat down on the wrong line, or your anger was subdued on the medium shot but boiling-hot on the close-up. Matching action is one of those tools one learns along the way. You want to give the editor a surfeit of possibilities and trust, really trust, that they will bend over backwards to put your best performance in their assembly. Having said all this, I sympathize with actors, and I've known many, who express indifference or impatience with the continuity department. These actors would rather be spontaneous than correct. Then there are those veteran actors I've worked with who find physical matching so oppressive they sedulously avoid making any extraneous movements. They will sit stoically at dinner scenes, take one bite on their opening line or drink one sip of "wine" and that's it, they then settle back into stillness, no dabbing of their lips with their napkin, no crossing of their arms, no gestures period and no matching action issues either. I've never been that actor. I'd rather mismatch and look alive. Let's face it, the editor is scouring the dailies for reactions, visual interest, you know, basic signs of life. We're making moving pictures after all. I'd rather be a presence worth cutting back to than the man not eating, not drinking, not living.

D.W. Brown: Aside from acting skills, what are the most important traits that will make a director or producer want to hire you again?

Peter MacNicol: A director wants to remember an actor as someone who did the job professionally, on time, and ready to work. They want someone who brings light and life to the party instead of moodiness and need. They want an actor who treats the entire crew with respect. They want an actor who knows his lines to the point of finding more in those words than even the writer did. They want actors to be prepared, but not inflexible. Directors appreciate our passion and our advocacy for our parts. But when advocacy turns to annoying self-interest, we leave lasting negative impressions. Directors are the busiest people on the set with ceaselessly churning minds. Their time is precious. So if an actor raises a problem with the director, that actor should also propose a solution. The world is full of actors, but fewer directors. It's a hard job to get and a harder job to keep getting. Those that got it fought for it. Now that they have it, they want to be allowed to do it.

D.W. Brown: What do you do when you disagree with your director?

Peter MacNicol: This is a hard one. Artistic differences do arise. Sometimes a director's suggestions sit awkwardly with us, and it feels like when we implement them we're playing the director's notes instead of playing our character. It feels like tissue rejection after an unsuccessful transplant, the direction seems grafted on to us. When we can't bend the director to our way of seeing or feeling the scene, it's vital that we not let our pride get pulled into the discussion. That's always a bad idea. This is a time for making fewer points, not more points. Look, the truth is, there's no perfect solution to these encounters, but there is one workable approach and it's this: I always feel that the director owes me my own "try" at it. And when I feel I've given it my best shot, I will let him make his adjustment. But I need the director's adjustment to make more than just intellectual sense to me. I also need it to make "emotional" sense; if I can't feel the rightness of the note, I can't play it, period. And if I try and fail, then I haven't pleased anybody, me, the director, the audience, but the failure is all mine to live with. Having said this, I want to stress that I try my level-best to pull off whatever it is that my director is asking of me once they've filmed me doing it my way. Do I risk them not using my takes? Yes, but after all, this is a collaborative medium. As I said, this a hard question. There are times, mercifully rare in my experience, where it becomes clear to me that the director and I really see things fundamentally differently. These experiences are among the most challenging an actor can face. You don't want to resist your bosses and get fired or be branded "difficult." Neither do you want to fail in the part and leave behind lasting negative impressions with the director, the producers, the writers, even the casting director. On these occasions, anger and panic can sit just below the surface. The temptation to quit rises up. At this point you have two options before you. You can give in to the director's vision or stick to your own. It's high stakes poker either way. I've done both and, if I'm being honest, neither feels satisfying.

D.W. Brown: How do you deal with the nerves?

Peter MacNicol: Well, for me, I try and keep foremost in my mind that acting is more than the intersection of commerce and art. Yes, it's both of those, but it's also one thing more, it's "playtime." To be precise, acting is that game we played as kids, dress up! It's very easy for children to play, but sometimes very hard for adults, unless those adults can somehow manage to summon up the inner child to do their playing for them. Granted, it's a game where mistakes cost money, but the child doesn't think about that. Nor can we when we're acting. We must do as they do on the playground, shed our punishing self-editors and give way to this managed madness that is our profession, where we paint our faces, dress up and cavort around in plywood rooms with three walls and no ceilings. And because it's taken me a lifetime to learn all this, I can add one more thing about "the game." On the actor's playground, the "kids" having the most fun are the ones who come out on top for they are the loosest and the most in tune with the enchanted land of the subconscious where ideas grow on trees. Whereas the actors working so carefully and cautiously to get everything right are often the losers. Why? Because fear of making mistakes kills the fun, tightens the body, freezes the imagination, and ruins the game.

....

GREGG CHAMPION INTERVIEW
Director (*The Cowboy Way; Short Time; Miracle Run*), producer.

D.W. Brown: What kind of things do you like from actors?

Gregg Champion: I like actors to ask questions. I like them to ask how they might approach the role. This way I get a sense for how they might be thinking about their part. You know, every actor has such a different approach. Maybe they're a stage actor, like Dianne Weise. I was very excited to work with her, and she was very prepared for her character, but she wanted me to tell her where to walk and where to stand and I realized that that was her background in coming from the stage. She really liked to be told where to stand and where to move. But there are actors who can be very different about that, actors who really like free range.

D.W. Brown: Yes, there are actors who can resent being told too much how to move.

Gregg Champion: Yes. Every person has a key to what their particular security might be in terms of approaching a role and so I love it when they have a lot of questions. Not all directors feel that way, I know, so an actor may have to feel that out, but I want to know what they're interested in developing. A lot of times an actor won't see the entire arc of the film. They see it in perhaps a more narrow particular way. What I really hope for with an actor is that they are engaged, that they've thought some things through. Whether it's what the character might wear, how they might behave in a certain circumstance, something contextual, or maybe a back story that isn't even in the script. I worked with Ellen Burstyn who is a wonderful actress. And she had about twenty questions for me which had nothing to do immediately with the script, but these things really informed how she approached the role.

D.W. Brown: If you were to try to articulate what makes someone powerful on screen, what would you say that is?

Gregg Champion: It's the quality of the person. Gravitas. It has to do with a certain presence, a restraint in the performance. When I think of the guys like Robert Redford, Steve McQueen, Paul Newman, they didn't have to say that much because it was in their presence. It was in their bearing. They never overplayed anything. A lot of the greats, if anything, they're always understated.

D.W. Brown: A level of trust.

Gregg Champion: Yes, exactly.

D.W. Brown: How much do you think actors should be aware of continuity?

Gregg Champion: Well, in a lot of comedy, I think actors are served to just mostly let it all go, to just do their thing. On the other hand, with other kinds of material, that can be a problem. I was working on a movie called *Stakeout* with Aidan Quinn, and he was a very method kind of actor, a great fan of Marlon Brando and James Dean and he emulated their work. One day Aidan, myself, and John Badham were going to lunch and we walked by the cutting room, which was right next to the stage, and the great editor Tom Rolf was working there, a very crusty guy, and he yelled out "Aidan, get in here!" And we walked in and we stood there and Rolf read Aidan the riot act. He said, "Nothing matches! I can't cut any of this together. You're doing one kind of value here and something totally different over here." And Aidan stood there stunned. And he said, "Oh, my God. I thought matching was just having the glass in the right hand or not. I didn't know I needed to match my performance. That explains it! That explains why my good stuff doesn't show up in the movies I do." It was like this big epiphany for him.

D.W. Brown: What kind of atmosphere do you like on the set?

Gregg Champion: I particular like a very calm set. I like to know what's going on and be in touch with everything. But I know directors who like a very chaotic set. It's just a matter of choice and it's not always the choice of the director either, of course. Some actors can have a hard time in television where time is very short. It's always a rush and you get very few takes. You might only get two or three takes in television. I think what's important, in the whole process, is to learn to love the imperfections. That there will be this human element. And I think what's most important politically is that people feel listened to.

....

MIMI LEDER INTERVIEW
Director (*ER*, Emmy for Best Director twice; *Deep Impact; The Peacemaker*), producer.

D.W. Brown: There are times when you can be working under a tremendous time pressure. Can you speak to how an actor can best deal with that pressure of the ticking clock?

Mimi Leder: It's your job to come in there and bring it. I've had times when I'm shooting an all-nighter and the sun is coming up and it's going to ruin the shot, and it's like, "OK, Baby, it's now or never. Let's get it." There are times when you have to tell the actor, "This is it. We just have to get it done." And the actor has to trust that it's going to be all right.

D.W. Brown: They can't let themselves get tormented over the fact that it's not being done the way they thought it was going to be done, and in doing that, cut themselves off from what can be done.

Mimi Leder: Exactly. And sometimes, the result is even better because it is spontaneous and isn't so thought out. If something is thought out, I don't ever want to see that. Sometimes an actor can get too "in their head."

D.W. Brown: This can be a real challenge, though, can't it? When under pressure we tend to go into our heads and try and work it out, but that cuts you off from the spirit, which is the thing you're really trying to capture on camera.

Mimi Leder: Right. Well, you just have to keep the spirit close to your heart. Even in the time crunch and with all the pressure. Always keep your eye on what the scene is about.

D.W. Brown: You've worked with some great actors, Mimi. What would you say makes them distinct?

Mimi Leder: I would say what's distinct about great actors is that they are really smart. And, what's very interesting to me is there are some actors who aren't necessarily extremely intelligent in, say, their IQ level, but they can come off brilliant when they're acting. I think it's their connection to the truth. Their ability to deeply tell the truth through their character.

....

PETER CORNWELL INTERVIEW

Director (*The Haunting in Connecticut, Mercy, Hemlock Grove [TV]*).

D.W. Brown: Most of your stuff has been in the thriller or horror genre. What aspect of acting is most important for a performer working in that genre?

Peter Cornwell: You want to believe that they're experiencing what they're experiencing. When you're portraying a scary situation, the actors really need to be scared. The audience will only be as scared as the actors are. I think you can look at the history of scary movies and see this. All the really good ones have great acting in them. You don't want to detect that they're acting. With a horror movie you're trying to make it seem like a documentary most of the time. I think an actor is an emotional bridge into the story and the more special the circumstances, the more dependent you are on having actors create that. The more real they feel, the more real it is for us. I think if you want emotion in the story you have to believe the actor is really feeling it. I remember you said that if an actor wanted to relate to playing a vampire they might imagine they haven't had water in a great while, and that could connect them to thirst with the kind of reality you want.

D.W. Brown: Yes. And I suppose, unlike with a play, you could get to that place by going without water for a while and then imagine that the throat you were going to bite would quench that real thirst.

Peter Cornwell: Yeah. Shelley Duval said that she was really traumatized making *The Shining*. Even with the B movie type of scary movie, the good ones like *Texas Chainsaw Massacre* I think have effective acting. They shot really long hours and that girl really was traumatized. Whatever the actor has to do to get themselves there, there's really no substitute for creating that emotional reality.

. . . .

MARTHA COOLIDGE INTERVIEW

Director (*Valley Girl, Real Genius, Lost in Yonkers*), writer, producer.

D.W. Brown: Rehearsal time is often a problem in movies and television. What advice do you have for an actor who has to deal with that?

Martha Coolidge: Rehearse. Don't worry about SAG (the Screen Actor's Guild) and the rules about rehearsal, get together with the other actors and the director, if possible, and rehearse. Do it on the weekends, do it whenever you can. Nobody cares, but your career is depending on you being good. You're judged as an actor by what you do, not by how the production was set up.

D.W. Brown: Right. They're not going to run a little script notification along the bottom of the screen while you're acting describing how you were limited in the amount of time you had to put your performance together.

Martha Coolidge: Exactly. You're going to rise or fall by the quality of your skill, and that's no joke. One of the worst parts of the business is how little rehearsal time there is. And an actor comes in to the production by himself, and what is he going to do? Here's what happens: If you have not rehearsed the way you would normally rehearse a play, then you have not set how you're going to be dealing with the blocking and the use of the props. So, what you generally do is you do a master and then, unfortunately, the actors have to confine themselves to what was done in the master. Tying a behavior to a word is not a bad thing. However, memorizing it that way, if you haven't had a chance to rehearse, you can have a problem if things get changed and you've made such a strong association with the prop and the line, then when you don't have the prop you're likely to forget your line. It gets all tied together. Which is why it's a bad idea to memorize in association with a behavior. It's always easier to do behaviors that are natural to you because they will be second nature and easier to add or subtract. You can certainly try things, you can ask if you could have a cup of coffee in the scene. There's nothing wrong with that. But if they ask you to give it up you have to be ready to work another way. All kinds of preparation an actor can do by himself, but not the stuff that's in conjunction with the group, and that's why I say get together with the other actors. Take it upon yourself to rehearse with them. I think there's a tremendous lack of understanding about how much work goes into acting in a movie. Because in the movie it's done piece by piece and that's, in its way, a kind of blessing because you can concentrate on each thing as it's coming up. But that doesn't mean that as you approach each day you're not considering the whole arc of your character. This can be very difficult to accomplish when it's shot out of order.

D.W. Brown: Yes, and you can look at a single page of a script that's going to be shot and say, "Well, it's just a couple lines of dialogue I'll be delivering," and forget how important each thing you do is to the whole.

Martha Coolidge: That's exactly right. The dialogue is only a compass. It only gives you an indication of what the scene might be about. The dialogue might actually not even be anything like what the scene is really about. It's not the dialogue. You can be in a movie and be on camera just about every second and not even speak that much and you're the lead of the movie, it's your story.

D.W. Brown: What would you say is the single most important thing in acting for a camera?

Martha Coolidge: Relaxation. That you can stay relaxed and in the moment. It's far more critical than being imaginative because at least it's real. The camera shoots what's real. So, to me, when I say real that includes being intelligent about what is real and figuring out a way to get there.

JERRY ZUCKER INTERVIEW

Director (*Airplane!, Ghost, Rat Race*), writer, producer.

D.W. Brown: What is it that you think makes a film performance effective?

Jerry Zucker: I think there's nothing more important than believability. Especially comedy, where believability is more important than people think. The context is hugely important in comedy, and I think the believability is really funny. I think the great comic actors are often just great actors. Even when they're broad, they don't let on that they think they're funny.

D.W. Brown: Maybe you've heard this, but there was a sitcom, I don't remember which one, but they had a sign on the wall, "No winking."

Jerry Zucker: Oh, that's great. That's what it is. I think, in any role, you have to bring it up from a deeper place. It shouldn't all just come from the mouth. That's the problem with a lot of acting that you see in auditions, for instance. There's nothing behind it. And, by the way, that's probably why a lot of great actors have had a lot of pain in their lives. Because I don't know that somebody who's been loved from day one and lived with just a lot of happiness and has no issues can go out there and give a great performance filled with pain.

D.W. Brown: What kinds of directions have you found to be most helpful with actors?

Jerry Zucker: I like to empower actors. Give them confidence and make them feel they're contributing. I don't want them to worry that they're not doing it right or that they're not pleasing me. Sometimes after I've got a bunch of takes and I think I've probably got what I need, I'll tell the actor, "Great, now do it again and don't pay attention to anything I've said." And that will usually be the best take, or at least a very solid take. And what happens is, it's not like they go off on their own way, they still somehow unconsciously incorporate what we discussed beforehand, but maybe not so specifically.

D.W. Brown: I think it's the feeling that, if they wanted to, they could go off in a different direction that changes everything.

Jerry Zucker: Exactly. Essentially what you're saying is, "Don't worry about getting it right." A lot of times I think the best directions are very simple. Once I was directing Patrick Swayze (in *Ghost*) and I was going into, I don't remember what it was, but it was some long-winded direction, and I started going into this thing about his past and his character and what he always dreamed about and I was going on and on with all this stuff that I thought was going to help and I finally stopped and Patrick said, "So, what you mean is faster and louder." And I had to go, "Yes, that is essentially what I want." And that amused me, but I think "faster and louder" is sometimes a great direction. Faster is always good. I know a lot of directors have said that they always do one take that is really fast. Because things tend to play slower on film than they might feel live. You might be looking at the monitor, and somehow it doesn't matter on the set and you're in the moment of it, and then in the editing room you're snapping your fingers wanting it to go faster. And, sometimes "louder" is helpful as a direction because it makes people put themselves out there more.

D.W. Brown: Aside from the actual performance, what is it about a particular actor that will make you want to keep working with them?

Jerry Zucker: Well, of course, it is mostly that confidence that someone gives me that they're going to be good in a specific part. That trumps everything. But I would rather work with actors who are cooperative. I love being challenged. I love actors who have opinions about things, but there's a way to do it without being confrontational or adversarial. That's a big deal to me. People who are all about the work. It's just a matter of human kindness more than anything. You know, if you're going to sign up to do a movie, you should see the director's other work and ask him questions about the movie you're getting into, and then trust. You know it's really that thing, "in for a penny, in for a pound." You really have no other choice.

D.W. Brown: The actor's passion should be woven into enthusiasm for the entire project. Not just their own performance.

Jerry Zucker: Yeah, it's a lot of work and everyone should just dig in and have a good time. And by "good time" I don't mean that everybody has to be joking around and having fun, but moviemaking should be enjoyable. It's a privilege. It's a real privilege.

D.W. Brown: A little gratefulness, maybe.

Jerry Zucker: You know what, that's really it. Everyone should be grateful. I just think everybody should go into it feeling they're lucky to be in this business.

....

ROB COHEN INTERVIEW
Director (*Fast And Furious, DragonHeart, Daylight*), writer, producer.

D.W. Brown: What's a major point you'd like to share with actors acting for the camera?

Rob Cohen: There's an insidious logic in the editing room that isn't apparent on the soundstage, and it can be shocking to actors when they see the cut of the film. Even though you're the guy playing the friend or the girl and you may have your own world and your own character traits, the focus probably has to be on the lead, no matter how good a moment of your performance is. Ultimately, as a filmmaker, you have the one assignment and that's to have this scene convey the complexity of your main characters.

D.W. Brown: You're saying that it's possible that the more remarkable the moment you create as an actor in those supporting parts, the more distracting it could be from where the attention of the audience needs to be for the story.

Rob Cohen: Yes. The director loves you, he hugs you and tells you "that was transcendent!" Now you come back six months later with these words in your head about how transcendent you were, thinking you can't wait to see your scene, and then you see your scene, and, if it's still in, then there's all the stuff there with the chair, and the inserts, and then the other character is featured and only half of that is played on your face. So, half is on other stuff and half of what's left is played on the other character's face, and you end up with only a quarter of what you were thinking was going to be shown. When you see that stuff in the editing room long after the lights and the excitement of the set, you understand all of a sudden what Buddhism tries to teach us: it's not all about us. Give it up. You've got to create these performances because that's what you've chosen to do in your life, and where they go you cannot be attached to. As difficult as that is, you never know where they're going to go.

D.W. Brown: What's interesting here, Rob, is I think you're offering something beyond just solace for an actor disturbed by the nature of the cut. It seems to me, this is also advice on how an actor can improve for themselves what shows up in the final product. If they want to be happier with what goes on in the editing room, they should seek to understand the part they're playing in the story as a whole, not just their personal contribution.

Rob Cohen: You're given three scenes, six pages, and you're going to shoot for a day and a half, maybe two days. What do they need from you in those three scenes that is going to be best for the film? Not best for your technique and not for your preconceived ideas, but, "What am I about in this film?" "What am I doing in this movie?" You want to be a fully developed character, that's the right instinct, but the wrong instinct is assuming that you're a fifty-fifty partner. And the set is designed to make you feel like you're a fifty-fifty partner. But you are not a fifty-fifty partner and that's what the editing room will show you. Nobody's a fifty-fifty partner. The film is the hundred percent owner, it controls everything. And when you force your ideas onto the movie, very often you're fighting what the movie is really telling you. Even the director can fall prey to this. In the end the film owns itself. You have to understand that it is this organic thing that starts to breathe and it's all of our jobs to midwife it.

D.W. Brown: It's a sensibility for making the piece a success in its entirety, and that only as a function of that can you stand out. You may have to get your head around the fact that, for this game, you're a shooting guard, not a point guard.

Rob Cohen: It's very appropriate to use sports metaphors in thinking about an actor's role in a movie. With an athlete, if he's built a certain way and has a certain kind of athletic prowess, then that's why he's there and what he should be doing. He won't play a different position. There are some actors who have a greater flexibility based on their physical and temperamental aspects, but they must ask themselves what the team needs.

D.W. Brown: Thinking about the genre might help. Whether it's a light comedy or a detective story and what kind of specific types of roles fill the gaps in this genre. I suppose, if you're playing an eccentric character who's supposed to be an obstacle for the main character, then some personality quirks might be called for, if it's interesting to have the lead forced to negotiate their way around this multifaceted person. But, otherwise, a lot of extraneous character detail is going to be clutter.

Rob Cohen: Yeah, it's about staying pure within yourself, but knowing intelligently how that character is most going to be successful for the film itself. With the purity of an artist you have to be detached with what happens to what you do.

D.W. Brown: You've done a lot of action pictures. Would you say there's anything special about acting in an action film that an actor should be aware of?

Rob Cohen: I think you have to be aware of what kind of action picture it is. A superhero type of action film is one kind of action, and then you have a different kind of action that has comedy or if it's straight, hard-core action. You need to pitch your performance to that level where the acting and the action don't fight each other. If you're, like, dead serious that you're really getting shot at and you're sincerely scared, but you're in something more tongue-in-cheek, that's not going to blend. There are levels of reality.

D.W. Brown: That's very interesting, because I'm sure when an actor is shooting some of these action sequences with you they can feel the genuine danger of what they're doing, and yet the style of the film is such that their character carries themselves with a confidence that, in this world they're inhabiting, it's impossible for them to be seriously injured or killed.

Rob Cohen: Oh yeah, if you're in one of my mic-rigs and you're being driven ninety to one hundred miles an hour down the street and you're shooting out a window you can get yourself pretty jacked up. You need to know where the tonality of the action is in order to integrate your performance with it.

D.W. Brown: When you work with seasoned actors, you see how they have their thing down. You see they've found things that work.

Rob Cohen: Oh, yeah. They have this ability to push away all of the superficial awareness about the moviemaking apparatus, the noise. They have a way of pushing that away. The camera is like this visual MRI, it really picks up who people are. There are no secrets from it once it's turned on the person. If they're guarded, it sees that they're guarded. It can even see what they might be guarding. If people are letting it hang out excessively, it reveals that as another form of defense. The performances we register as the truest are the ones where the people are being and not acting. It's where they're in line with what the film needs them to be. They are being that thing without thought, without too much control or apparent premeditation. We talk about discovery, we talk about that freshness of really seeing something happen, moments where what the film means, it hits the actor like, boom! You see that meaning coming into their minds or their hearts in that moment, and you see that complete and utter possession by the character and you go, "Wow. That was true."

D.W. Brown: It's really about when that event lands, isn't it?

Rob Cohen: When the camera is there and you're not thinking about it and something just hits you and you react to it consistent with how you designed the character . . . but it isn't like anything has happened to your thinking. It's where the character meets the world.

. . . .

JOHN PATRICK SHANLEY INTERVIEW
Director (*Doubt*), writer (*Moonstruck* — Academy Award; *Doubt* — Tony, Pulitzer, Academy Award).

D.W. Brown: You worked with Meryl Streep who, pretty much by consensus, is regarded as the finest actor of our generation. What was your experience with her like?

John Patrick Shanley: She likes to be in costume. The first day Meryl was knitting. Then Amy (Adams) and Meryl were knitting. She taught Amy to knit. And I would be reading a newspaper. And we would sit together for fairly long periods of time on the set while they were lighting. I remember the First A.D. at one point saying: "They have a trailer." But, I knew that the reason they were there was there was a collaborative, nonverbal process. The director lives in the atmosphere and so if you're a sensitive actor you're very absorbent. You can sit around without saying, "You should do this," or "I had this idea." Just sit around together. There is a communal absorption of energy that gets you on the same page that can be really useful. With Meryl, you can tell, she has this process to find a way to work that is enjoyable. Now, having said that, she's a trouper and if she finds herself in a war, she will take up arms, and she will fight that war committedly, but her vast preference is to find a way of working that nourishes her as a human being and makes her ongoing life a pleasure. Amy had what I think of as the benefit of youth. In between takes, Amy's chatting away with the crew and everyone and then it's time and she walks over and breaks into tears and does the big scene. She has that kind of fluidity. But at a certain point your natural facility abandons you so you become introspective. And then you have to develop a second act of technique to deal with that. And Meryl was like on the fourth act of her technique. She was much quieter and serious, while still being social. She found a different balance. So, with Amy, she was very easy to fall in and out of character, while Meryl had this steady, steady attack, a concentration, a contemplation really, on what she was doing. Actors who can call forth their characters when needed and retire them when not needed are the most fun to work with, but it's not always possible. By the way, Meryl Streep is the most grounded, together person you will ever meet.

D.W. Brown: Yes, I use her as, if not giving full lie to, then at least a very clear exception to the idea that tremendous talent has to be born of tremendous personal turmoil. I saw an interview with her where she was asked if she would like to do a play and she said that she'd love to do theater, but the required nights away from home would be unacceptable because she had two teenage daughters. The interviewer thought he was merely confirming the situation when he then asked, "Your daughters would be upset to have you away that much?" and she said, "No, they'd love to have me away that much, but I'm not going to be."

John Patrick Shanley: Ah ha ha, yeah. She is just terrific.

D.W. Brown: What do you think the job of the actor is, essentially?

John Patrick Shanley: Well, you know an actor is comprised of many things, and only one of those parts is a real problem. That is their ego. The ego is very necessary to wake up the inner psyche. But, basically, with acting you're replacing your ego with somebody else's ego. Everything else is you. Your consciousness, your intelligence, your facilities, your shortcomings. The one thing that is not helpful is your ego. You can't play your career, you can only play the role that you're handed. Get out of the way and play it.

D.W. Brown: You've been intimately exposed to both stage and film acting. What are the essential differences in those styles of acting?

John Patrick Shanley: One of the differences is that stage actors must allow for the contribution of the audience. The audience is a character. The stage actor makes room for this character to express its response. On film, the actor must subtly include the camera in his or her performance, and this inclusion is different. The film actor must perform a visual dance of revelation and withholding. It's a conversation with the lens, complete with secrets unrevealed. If the film actor holds on to no secret, it's a failed performance. Whereas a stage actor has to adjust their performances to include the audience, a film actor doesn't have to do that. They might just be playing for the director.

AN ACTOR'S MANIFESTO

....

Enter the fictional world with a sense of belonging, like a fish in water, seeking closer contact with the events of the imaginary at the height of Universal Truth, freely responding with an expectation you will be intimately received. Let it all flow in and all flow out. Delight in what is humorous and take everyone seriously, finding nothing unreasonable and little confusing, stillness and silence your sacred foundations. Play without thinking.

Be a tuned-in, vulnerable egomaniac with massive empathy. Release yourself from concern about how clever or put together you look, aware that dissociation and anticipation will constantly be corrupting you to appear that way. Entertain without apology, celebrating the primitive and the sublime both, doing interesting things and letting interesting things be done to you. Combine humility for your craft with audacity in performance. Aspire to be known, especially those parts of yourself you think most shameful. Care and don't care. You have nothing to prove.

All the while you are applying your maximum level of concentration to what's taking place within the imaginative sphere, permit another aspect of your nature to be conscious of your audience as an open-hearted, fellow traveler being lead by you into the beautiful and terrible, unknown world of the play. Accept the responsibility of being this sacrificial tour guide knowing that, not only will the audience perceive the journey differently than you do, but aspects of your experience should properly be kept private from them.

Live with the same ferocity and abandon you did when you were a very young child and carve deeply into make-believe with specificity. Strive always for more ease and simplicity in everything you do. Execute your plan and follow inspiration, but do not believe any conscious expressions of your personality have merit; your ideas and moods are contaminants and obstructions to the flow of the truth. Shut up and get out of the way.

Before performing, daydream vivid experiences that your character has had with the other characters (and objects) so they automatically dictate your behavior in their presence. Visualize images of your Objectives being gained or lost so they will live in you and be stimulated by your successes and failures. Allow that your Objective might only be to have your experience appreciated by someone (often a situation's outrageousness), and be open to responding and delivering lines while profoundly stunned.

Determine the ways that your character is different from yourself (if any) and seek to habituate the way they speak, move, the functioning of their faculties, and the methodologies they use to get what they want. Adjust your responses to events appropriate for your character (where necessary), making these things either more or less strange and significant than they would be for you, then connect to the resulting Objectives at their greatest degree of consequence to your character's needs and Life Drive. Be conscious where you should be conscious (in your homework before acting and on the moments while acting) and unconscious where you should be unconscious (abandon knowingness).

Know what you're saying and express its core truth, speaking to hearts, not to heads. Every line of dialogue you utter must serve your excellent Action, and you must not permit the seduction of the values seemingly inherent in the words to distort the thrust of what you're doing (usually impressing upon, relieving, or seducing). Always be closing. At the same time, your Actions in the playing should be constantly infused, and even challenged, by each new event, including the emotional associations brought about by any historical material introduced by others or your own recounting. Keep connected to your Objective and play the moments.

When preparing for a role, study and apply yourself to the aspects of the character's life in all its important details in order to honor the fullness of their humanity, and, no matter how wretched they appear to others, you must believe every character you portray to be someone you have to live up to. Dare that your audience will confuse you with your character . . . indeed, wish it!

Consider yourself a student of the human condition in general (rich/poor, brutal/lovely, large gestures/tiny gestures) and, specifically, how it expresses itself in you. Be acquainted with the great works of art and those who created them. Learn from, and copy freely, the techniques of the masters and the novice next to you, alike. Everything, particularly what you cannot pin down with a name, nourishes you.

Because your job is the expression of peak human vitality,

it will be necessary for you to keep your instrument in excellent health. Because you will need your psyche as pure as possible to concentrate and make available your gifts, you must keep your spirit uncluttered by personal turmoil. To this end, cultivate a just, lively, grateful nature, and a gentle superiority over misfortune. Do your work and *let life happen.*

You are part of a tradition that goes back to the earliest beginnings of civilization and has consistently provided a moral compass leading to improvement in the quality of life on earth. It is your responsibility to honor those who have come before you, just as you are entitled to expect the best of those who follow.

CHARISMA REVEALED

....

It's said of some actors that "the camera loves them," that they have "star quality." Performers blessed with this charm make us feel we know them and they induce us to live vicariously through their experiences. We want something from them, but we don't know what it is. The very charismatic can make us feel both large and small, pleased and aching, simultaneously. I'm guessing you'd like some of that quality when you're on camera, and here's my best advice for how to get it: Be very average.

It's my belief performers display that kind of magnetism, not by being so freakishly different from the rest of us, but because they so closely hit the universal mark for how we all truly are in essence. It's the reason some of our most captivating actors (Jimmy Stewart, Jack Lemmon, Tom Hanks, etc.) get referred to as an "everyman." We sense their values are close to that sweet spot for what we average as a culture.

I developed my theory of charisma from studying koinophilia, the term for the evolutionarily preference animals have for mates with a minimum of unusual features. We know when people are presented with computer-processed composite faces, using morphed photographs of actual faces, that an image created from the greatest number of faces—the most average face—is considered the most attractive. This favoring, observable in the extended looks of infants only six months of age, is clearly an instinctive preference for common features proven to be successful. I've simply extrapolated this phenomenon to be applicable to human personality traits as well.

There may be different personality types who have different I.Q.s and Life Goals. They may range from Tom Hanks in *Forrest Gump* to Tom Cruise in *Jerry McGuire*, but all charismatic characters hold very similar, basic orientations with respect to what they feel is good behavior, bad behavior, and borderline behavior.

Charismatic characters are capable of doing something sinful, certainly, but they nevertheless feel exactly how bad it is in relation to the norm. If they act with cruelty, for instance, this wickedness hurts them in its commission as much as any good person, but is endured because it either serves the greater good, is superseded by a powerful craving, or because it delivers a masochistic delight in itself, like the sting from a shot of whiskey.

The charismatic individual exhibits a balance (their Brown Rating) between caring too much or too little in five spheres of ethics and the expression of seven personality traits.

Ethics
1. Fairness (concern for justice)
2. Loyalty (value on faithfulness)
3. Purity/Sanctity (desiring cleanliness and holiness)
4. Respect (deference for the pecking order and tradition)
5. Safety (avoidance of injury to oneself and others)

Personality traits
1. Adventurousness (enthusiasm for action)
2. Consistency (steadiness and honesty)
3. Frugality (use of resources)
4. Humor (delight in absurdities, especially about oneself)
5. Scope (sense of magnitude, humility)
6. Tempo (rhythm of experience)
7. Vulnerability (emotional sensitivity)

What this means is you must not seek to be different by being on the fringe, but rather by being so especially central. You are a totally unique thing in the history of this universe, that's a given, but you share with your intended audience a current life force. To really shine you must work to be in unity with that. The attainment of the proper condition is rather how Rumi spoke of love when he said, "Your task is not to seek love, but merely to remove the barriers within yourself you have built against it."

The truth is there are many artists who assume a charismatic persona in performance they do not genuinely possess in life (seen in singers who even adopt a different accent when they sing), because they intuit how this created incarnation will better connect them with their audience. If you need to do that—to take on the aspect of a man of the people, a tuned in, primal, archetype vessel for personhood, no matter the character work you then overlay on top of that—do it.

Go to the theater. Not just to study the acting (as if that weren't enough), but to sense how a crowd responds to things presented in a fiction. An audience in a theater enters into a kind of sacred pact, and sitting there with them (or, of course, performing) you will become educated about what they are like according to the better angels of their nature. From the collective exclamations of approval and groans of disapproval, you learn and affirm the deep average response of that society. Being exposed to various kinds of group laughter teaches you the dimensions of present-day humor.

An audience tends to be smarter than any single member of it. This is called the "wisdom of crowds" and is probably why civilizations moving toward enlightenment have placed a significant value on theater. I'm afraid you're just not going to get the same effect watching your little handheld screen by yourself. The influence exerted on an individual by the power of an audience responding to fictional events can align them to values previously distorted by an insular upbringing.

With a little such encouragement it's possible your natural inclinations, which are naturally much more consistent with the charismatic average, can reassert themselves and—free again as you came into this world—you will be charismatic. Not by working to be different, but by being true to your deepest self. Let me say this again: whether it's a classic or something new, conventional or avant garde, writ large or writ small, big theater, small theater . . . *go to the theater.*

GLOSSARY

....

Abby Singer: The next-to-the-last shot of the day.

above the line (also used: "below the line"): The people who contribute to the creative aspect of a project and their related costs; including (but not limited to) the screenwriter, the actors, the director, and the producers.

action: The specific thing being done, the objective of this moment, and how the character intends to achieve it.

"Action!" The signal to begin acting a scene.

ad-lib: To improvise words not in the text.

ADR (also called "looping"): Automatic Dialogue Replacement. When actors dub their own dialogue in a studio after a scene has been filmed.

apple box: Flat wooden boxes of varying sizes used as single-hand portable platforms.

arc shot: A shot where the camera moves in a circle around the actor(s).

aside: The act of breaking the fourth wall to speak to the audience. This dialogue is not heard by the other characters on stage, and is done as the action is unfolding, as opposed to narration of action seen as a flashback. The aside relationship to the audience is as someone who is a friend, although possibly slightly below oneself in authority.

Assistant Director(s) (aka A.D.): Person(s) responsible for coordinating and executing technical matters pertaining to logistics and personnel (titles are 1st A.D., 2nd A.D., Second Second, then Additional Second in descending order of authority).

"Back to one." A command to get ready to start a shot again from the beginning.

base camp: A place where most of a production's facilities can be maintained, usually set up as close as possible to the site of the majority of the filming.

Best Boy: Assistant to the head electrician, aka "Gaffer."

block shoot: To shoot a series of different scenes from one prepped angle, although perhaps changing costumes and set decoration (necessitating the actors then shoot their coverage out of sequence). Done for time efficiency.

blocking: Where an actor stands and what he does physically during a performance.

boat truck: Scenery on wheels.

boom (aka fish pole or fishing rod): A microphone on a pole.

breaking: Coming out of the performance so as to reveal the personality of the actor. (This is the worst sin, unless skit-playing where it is, within limits, permissible.)

broom: To remove something from the set.

a build: Anything that is made especially for the movie.

call sheet: A paper issued prior to the next day's shooting that details the scenes that will be filmed, the personnel required to film them, and when those personnel are expected to be at the location.

Camera Operator: The person responsible for the technical requirements of the camera itself, including the focus.

cans: A headset.

cheat: A move made solely to improve the visual presentation for an audience. (So named because it is a sacrifice that cheats the natural truth of the actor.)

chewing the scenery: An actor making a spectacle of himself at the expense of the production.

chiaroscuro: High-contrast lighting.

choker: A close-up with the actor's full head in frame.

clapper board, clap stick: A flat board held up to be filmed which makes a sound so that the editor can synchronize the sound and the picture. Usually has pertinent scene information on it.

clean: Shot without anyone or any thing in the foreground of the frame except for who and what is mainly featured.

"Clear the lens." A command to get out of the frame someone or some thing in particular—or everyone and everything in general—that is not meant to be in the shot.

closed: Positioned physically so that the front of the body and face of the actor cannot be clearly seen.

cloth: A large, unframed canvas.

coda: A final scene that wraps things up, often a flash forward.

continuity: The consistent take-to-take positioning of objects and the appearance of costume and the actor's physicality, as well as the points of vocal and emotional amplitude, so that multiple takes can be intercut and still create the impression of one continuum.

"Copy that." A declaration in response to a comment or a request that indicates it has been fully understood and will be properly attended to.

coverage: The total shots taken of a scene from various angles.

cowboy: The actors framed from the level of their hips to just above their heads.

Craft Services: People responsible for providing meals and snacks; also, often refers to a given area where snacks are available.

crane: A device for raising and lowering the camera.

crawl: A very slow movement of the camera.

crosscutting: Cutting back and forth from two different scenes as they unfold.

cue: Designated point for an actor to initiate speech or action.

cue card: The place where lines have been written out to be read during a performance.

"Cut!" The signal to stop a scene.

cutaway: A shot of something that can be inserted into the scene so that it can be broken up from one continuous sequence.

dailies (aka rushes): All of the material recorded on a given day.

day of days: A chart indicating what days of a production that specific actors will be working.

depth-of-field: The range from foreground to background in which the camera is in focus.

Director of Photography (aka D.P.): The person in charge of all the departments responsible for all aspects of cinematography (i.e., lighting, camera movement, lens, etc.).

dolly: A device to wheel the camera around.

dress to camera: To position the objects and the performers on a set so as to create the most favorable picture for the camera.

dropping cues: An actor not delivering the proper cue lines to a fellow actor.

Dutch: When the framing of the camera is not parallel with the horizon.

fifty-fifty: A scene where two actors are shot in profile looking directly at each other.

First Team: The actors who will be appearing on camera, as opposed to the "Second Team," aka their stand ins.

flag: Anything used to prevent light from spreading.

flats: Painted pieces of cloth on frames.

flies: The space above the stage.

fluffing: To stumble over words.

flying in: Applied to a prop or a piece of technical equipment necessary to execute a take that is presently on its way to the set.

foley: Appropriate, atmospheric sounds inserted in postproduction.

French reverse: Shooting a reverse without changing where the camera is placed, but rather having the other actor in the scene go there, perhaps changing the background to support the illusion that it is a different angle. Done to save time.

Gaffer (also a verb: to gaff): The person responsible for the lighting on the set, considered the chief electrician.

gist phrase: A phrase ad-libbed by an actor that represents the main thrust of what their character is saying in essence at this moment; useful to the actor for staying behaviorally on point and not being swayed by the sensibility of the words.

going up (or going dry): Forgetting your lines.

golden time: Working on Sundays or holidays, which for union members means increased pay.

green room: A common area backstage.

Greensman: The person responsible for maintaining plants or imitation plants.

Grip: The person who sets up equipment.

hair in the gate: Something on or near the camera lens creating an imperfection.

hand-held: A camera that is carried.

hero: A location or a large prop that is impressive. It often will be heavily featured in the film and so is usually given extra detail.

honeywagon: The vehicle or trailer that contains dressing rooms for the actors.

hoot: To walk away from the camera with one's face turned to the side so more of the face can be seen.

hot: Can refer to an individual object or an entire set, and indicates that the placement is exact and should not be tampered with.

insert: A brief shot of a small detail (e.g., the gun in the drawer, the key placed in the shirt pocket).

Jonesy deck: A platform that is constructed for elevating equipment and personnel.

jumping: Skipping sections of text by speaking future lines.

key light: The best light on stage for the face.

"Last looks!" A warning to the involved departments (e.g., make-up, costume, etc.) that they have a limited amount of time before shooting takes place.

lavalier (also lav): A wireless microphone worn by talent.

"Leave room for the scissors." A request to pause in dialogue or hold a physical action so that an editor's cut can be made at that moment.

Line Producer: The person responsible for the logistical organization of principal photography.

locked-off: When the camera is meant to remain in a fixed position; to be left alone.

loose: Framed with a degree of surrounding room, enabling an actor to move freely without risking going out of frame.

magic hour (also golden hour): The time of day close to sunset and sunrise when external lighting has a soft quality.

"Make the day." To shoot everything that was scheduled to be shot for that day.

mark: A spot where an actor should stand during a scene.

martini: The final take of the day or for the entire shoot.

master (also master shot): A wide-angle shot usually only used to give the viewer perspective for where the scene is taking place.

match: Maintaining from take to take the consistent positioning of objects and the appearance of costumes and the actor's physicality, as well as his or her points of vocal and emotional amplitude, in order to aid continuity.

meal penalty: Money paid to the performer for missing a meal or for not having one provided on schedule as per actor's union requirements.

MOS: To record the moving image only, without recording any sound (from "motor only shot").

moving on: Going to a new camera setup.

on the day: When at the location with the materials and personnel present and just about to, or actually doing, the shooting. (Might be used even in reference to later in the same day.)

oner: Meant to be seen in the final film as one continuous shot.

open position: The performer positioned so that the front of his or her body and face can be seen.

OTS: Over the shoulder, a dirty shot with another actor's shoulder and side of head in the frame.

overcrank: To shoot the film so that when shown it will appear in slow motion (as opposed to "undercrank" for fast motion).

per diem: Money paid for daily expenses.

pick-up: To shoot just part of a scene.

pick-up cues: The early initiation of an actor's speaking upon receiving delivery of their cue line.

"Places!" The command to take your position immediately prior to "Action!" being called.

post: All the work that will be done after principal photography.

POV: The camera shooting a character's point-of-view.

practical: An object that actually works (e.g., a light or radio that turns on and off by it's true switch).

Production Assistant (also P.A.): A general, all-purpose worker.

Production Designer: The person responsible for the overall look of the film.

production stills: Photographs of the production.

racking: To change the camera's focus from foreground to background or vice versa.

read: When an object is identifiable or the meaning of a behavior understandable to the audience.

re-shoots: Re-shooting scenes or adding entirely new scenes later as a fix.

reverses: Shooting in the opposite direction (as in getting coverage for the other part of a conversation).

riser: Any platform used to elevate a person or object.

room tone (also buzz track): The sound of a location when no one is speaking, recorded for later use in postproduction.

Script Supervisor (or "Scripty"): The person responsible for maintaining continuity and exact delivery of the written words; as well as notations on what shots have been filmed and their durations.

Second Unit: A crew that shoots footage of locations and action that will be used in the film, but which are usually incidental and often filmed without sound.

setup: A specific placement of the camera and the lighting.

sides: Pages taken from a script to hold just those scenes in hand; often for the purpose of auditioning.

slate (also "Slate!"): The clapper board itself; or that process of marking the sound on the film; what is called out following "Speed!" and prior to "Action!"

soft: Not in perfect focus.

sotto voce: As if in confidence, under one's breath.

"Speed!" Called out by the Sound Mixer as recording of sound has begun in good order; also may be called for when running good sound, as when a contaminating sound is no longer detected.

squib: An explosive packet used to create the effect of bullets striking objects and people.

stage door: The door at the rear or side exterior of a theater.

stage whisper: A breathy voice, projected loud enough to be completely intelligible, but that indicates intimacy.

Stand In (also Second Team): A person of the same dimensions and coloring as the actor who duplicates the movements to be performed so that technical adjustments (camera, lighting, etc.) may be made in preparation for the actor.

Steadicam: A carried mount for a camera that enables the person holding it to move freely and still maintain a fluid framing for the camera.

stepping on cues: Interrupting the other actor so that they are unable to finish their lines.

sticks: A tripod to hold the camera.

storyboard: Cartoons of the exact shots in the film.

strike: To remove something from the set, which would include the act of dismantling it if necessary.

tableau: Actors holding positions to create a given picture.

take: A filmed version of part or all of a scene.

talent: The actors.

Teleprompter: An electronic display for cue cards.

tight: When the framing is very close to the actor's body and, because of this, perhaps restricts their movements.

tracking (also trucking): Moving the camera with a dolly.

turn around: Giving less than twelve hours off for an actor before he or she is required to return to work.

turning around: Changing the camera setup to shoot the reverse angle.

Tweeny: A lighting fixture designed specifically to light the eyes.

upstaging: Any behavior that directs audience focus away from one player onto another. (A move upstage by one actor forces the other actors to give the audience the backs of their heads in order to look at this performer.)

video village: A place where monitors are set up to display what's being seen through the camera, and where personnel gather to watch playback of what's been shot.

"What's your twenty?" A request made over the telephone or a walkie-talkie for the listener to state their present location.

wild track: Recording sound without picture to be used by the editor.

Wrangler (usually prefaced by a specific animal species): The person responsible for the handling and performance of an animal or animals.

wrap: The moment at which all shooting for that day, or all shooting for an entire production, is considered finished.

ACKNOWLEDGMENTS

The incomparable Michael Wiese asked me to write this book and it is to him it is dedicated. He published my other two books and, when he heard I was teaching a master class on acting for the camera, we had a conversation about combining what I know on the subject with insights from gifted professionals. This resulted in the interviews with these wonderful people you find collected here, and my heartfelt thanks to all of them. Of course, going back further was my good fortune in having an association with Joanne Baron, generally considered one of the greatest acting teachers of the last hundred years. In addition to being cute, funny, kind, and my wife of thirty years, she's been willing to share some of her brilliance with me along the way. I'd also like to thank the dedicated instructors who work at our acting studio, along with the staff, including Robert Stallons for his proofreading of this book. Great thanks as well to the entire crew from Michael Wiese Productions, especially the amazingly gifted designer John Brenner for his cover, razor-sharp copyeditor David Wright, and Debbie Berne for her strong design work. More than anyone I have to thank the actors I've been privileged to know over the course of my life. They are a brave, impassioned, humane, and vulnerable group of crazy people, and the world is a much better place for them being in it.

 D. W. Brown is the author of the acclaimed book *You Can Act: A Complete Guide for Actors* and *2500 Years of Wisdom*. In addition to directing numerous theatrical productions, he wrote and directed the feature film *On the Inside* (starring Olivia Wilde and Nick Stahl) and the short films *One Clean Move, Chloe, The Need for Flowers,* and *Wrapper.* Mr. Brown has personally coached and trained such talent as Robin Wright, Leslie Mann, Olivia Wilde, Keanu Reeves, and Sam Raimi, and led seminars with Sean Penn, Sydney Pollack, Anthony Hopkins, Halle Berry, and Susan Sarandon. He is the head instructor of Los Angeles' premier acting school, The Joanne Baron/DW Brown Studio (www.baronbrown.com), which has been honored by such speakers as Tom Cruise, Tom Hanks, Dustin Hoffman, Robert DeNiro, and Pulitzer-winning dramatists John Patrick Shanley and David Mamet, as well as many other luminaries. He scuba dives, sculpts, his favorite indoor place is The Louvre, and his favorite outdoor place is Maui.

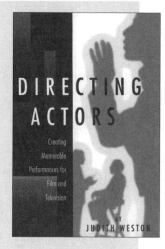